W9-BCY-417

Building
the
Learning
Organization

Building the Learning Organization

A Systems Approach to Quantum Improvement and Global Success

Michael J. Marquardt

Copublished with the American Society
for Training and Development

McGraw-Hill

New York   San Francisco   Washington, D.C.   Auckland   Bogotá
Caracas   Lisbon   London   Madrid   Mexico City   Milan
Montreal   New Delhi   San Juan   Singapore
Sydney   Tokyo   Toronto

Library of Congress Cataloging-in-Publication Data

Marquardt, Michael J.
    Building the learning organization : a systems approach to quantum
improvement and global success / Michael J. Marquardt.
        p.   cm.
    Includes index.
    ISBN 0-07-040534-4 (hardcover)
    1. Organizational learning. I. Title.
HD58.82.M37 1996
658.3'124—dc20   95-38979
                                             CIP

McGraw-Hill

A Division of The McGraw-Hill Companies

Copyright © 1996 by The McGraw-Hill Companies, Inc. All rights
reserved. Printed in the United States of America. Except as permitted
under the United States Copyright Act of 1976, no part of this publication may be reproduced or distributed in any form or by any means, or
stored in a data base or retrieval system, without the prior written permission of the publisher.

1 2 3 4 5 6 7 8 9 0 BKP/BKP 9 0 0 9 8 7 6 5

ISBN 0-07-040534-4

*The sponsoring editor for this book was Philip Ruppel, the editing supervisor
was Penny Linskey, and the production supervisor was Donald F. Schmidt. It
was set in Palatino by Victoria Khavkina of McGraw-Hill's Professional Book
Group composition unit.*

Printed and bound by Quebecor/Book Press.

McGraw-Hill books are available at special quantity discounts to use as
premiums and sales promotions, or for use in corporate training programs. For more information, please write to the Director of Special
Sales, McGraw-Hill, 11 West 19th Street, New York, NY 10011. Or contact your local bookstore.

 This book is printed on recycled, acid-free paper containing
a minimum of 50 percent recycled, de-inked fiber.

Contents

3. Building Dynamic Learning through the Organization   29

Preface

As we approach the twenty-first century, we are entering a new era in the evolution of organizational life and structure. The immense changes in the economic environment caused by globalization and technology have forced organizations to make significant transformations in order to adapt and survive in this new world.

The changes we are talking about are not just in external products, activities, or structures, but rather in the intrinsic way the organization operates: its values, mindset, even its primary purpose. Harrison Owens states this well in *Riding the Tiger: Doing Business in a Transforming World*. He writes: "There was a time when the prime business of business was to make a profit and product. There is now a prior, prime business, which is to become an effective learning organization. Not that profit and product are no longer important, but without continual learning, profits and products will no longer be possible. Hence the strange thought: the business of business is learning—and all else will follow."

Dinosaur-like organizations with slow, pea-sized brains will not survive in the faster, information-thick atmosphere of the new millennium. Greater size and thiker hides will not help these "old" companies compete with more agile and creative learning organizations. Or to cite another biological metaphor, putting quicker legs on a caterpillar will never enable the caterpillar to match the range and flexibility it achieves when it has been transformed into a butterfly.

Put very bluntly, organizations must learn faster and adapt to the rapid change in the environment or they simply will not survive. As in any transitional period, the dominant, dying species (i.e., nonlearning organization) and the emerging, more adaptive species (i.e., learning organization) exist side by side. Within the next ten years, I predict that only learning organizations will survive. Companies which do not become learning organizations will soon go the way of the dinosaur; they will die because they were unable to adjust to the changing environment around them.

Why Organizational Learning Is So Critical

The demands put on corporate America now require learning to be delivered faster, cheaper, and more effectively to a workplace and mobile work force more dramatically affected by daily changes in the marketplace than ever before.

And what are some of these critical issues facing today's corporations?

- Reorganization, restructuring, and reengineering for success, if not just survival
- Increased skills shortages, with schools unable to adequately prepare for work in the twenty-first century
- Doubling of knowledge every two to three years
- Global competition from the world's most powerful companies
- Overwhelming breakthroughs of new and advanced technologies
- Spiraling need for organizations to adapt to change

As Reg Revans, a pioneer of organizational learning notes, "Learning inside must be equal to or greater than change outside the organization or the organization is in decline, and may not survive."

Corporatewide, systemswide learning offers organizations the best opportunity of not only surviving but succeeding. As foreseen by leaders of the Rover Automotive Group in England, "The prospect that organizational learning offers is one of managing change by allowing for quantum leaps. Continuous improvement means that every quantum leap becomes an opportunity to learn and therefore prepare for the next quantum leap. By learning faster than our competitors the time span between leaps reduces and progress accelerates."

To obtain and sustain a competitive advantage in this new environment, organizations will have to learn better and faster from their successes and failures. They will need to continuously transform themselves into a learning organization, to become places where groups and individuals continuously engage in new learning processes.

Shoshana Zuboff, in her 1988 classic, *In the Age of the Smart Machine*, notes how today's organization may indeed have little choice but to become a "learning institution, since one of its principal purposes will have to be the expansion of knowledge—not knowledge for its own sake (as in academic pursuit), but knowledge that comes to reside at the core of what it means to be productive. Learning is no longer a separate activity that occurs either before one enters the workplace or in remote classroom settings. Nor is it an activity preserved for a managerial group. The behaviors that define learning and the behaviors that define being productive are one and the same. Learning is the heart of productive activity. To put it simply, learning is the new form of labor."

What Is the New Learning in Organizations?

There must, therefore, be a whole new mindset regarding the concepts of work and learning. Learning must take place almost as a by-product of people doing their work—in contrast to acquiring knowledge before performing a particular task or job. Learning in organizational settings in today's environment will represent a new form of learning in the following ways:

1. Learning is performance-based (tied to business objectives).
2. Importance is placed on learning processes (learning how to learn).
3. The ability to define learning needs is as important as the answers.
4. Organizationwide opportunities exist to develop knowledge, skills, and attitudes.
5. Learning is part of work, a part of everybody's job description.

The need for individuals and organizations to acquire more and more knowledge will continue unabated. But what organizations *know* takes second place to what and how quickly they can *learn*. Learning skills will be much more important than data. Penetrating questions will be much more important than good answers.

Emergence of Learning Organizations

Although the concept and importance of organizationwide learning can be traced in the research literature as far back as the 1940s, it was not until the 1980s that a few companies began realizing the potential power of corporate learning in increasing organizational performance, competitiveness, and success.

In the 1980s Shell started to consider organizational learning in relation to strategic planning. Teamwork and more extensive communications were seen as crucial factors in creating a more responsive, successful corporation. Shell spent 12 months experimenting with work groups and researching the implications of the learning organization concept. The company concluded that learning as an organization did indeed prove to be valuable both for strategic planning and corporate success: it had enabled Shell gain a year or two on its competitors.

In the early 1990s, the number of organizations committing themselves to becoming learning organizations increased. Organizations such as General Electric, Johnsonville Foods, Quad Graphics, and Pacific Bell in the United States; Sheerness Steel, Sun Alliance, and ABB in Europe; and Honda and Samsung in Asia were among the early pioneers.

The widespread attention directed to Peter Senge's *The Fifth Discipline* and feature articles on learning organizations in business publications, such as *Harvard Business Review, The Economist, Business Week, Fortune,* and *Asiaweek* has led many other companies to begin considering the process of transforming themselves into learning organizations.

Need for a Comprehensive Systems Approach to Defining Learning Organizations

Most organizations are struggling with becoming a learning organization; many others still don't grasp the importance of learning or how it actually works. As in the tale of the five blind men who described the elephant by the portion they could touch or feel, learning organizations have been described from only one aspect—the learning dynamics of teams or the organizational structure or the management of knowledge or the better application of new technology. Some organizations misconstrue even the part they are touching and confuse total-quality management or reengineering or better training as being the essence of organizational learning.

My experience over the past eight years with over 50 of the top learning organizations from all around the world, as well as my analysis of the hundreds of articles and books on learning organizations, has led me to conclude that the full richness of the learning organization incorporates five distinct subsystems—learning, organization, people, knowledge, and technology. Attempting to understand or become a learning organization without all five of these dimensions will lead to only a partial appreciation of the processes and principles necessary to move from a nonlearning to a learning organization.

This book will present each of the necessary five subsystems and how they interface and complement each other. The core subsystem of the learning organization, of course, is learning—at the levels of individual, group, and organization, with the skills (or disciplines as Peter Senge refers to them) of systems thinking, mental models, personal mastery, team learning, and shared vision. Each of the other subsystems—organization, people, knowledge, and technology—are required to enhance and augment the quality and impact of learning on a corporatewide basis.

Overview of Book

Chapter 1 assesses the changing social, political, and economic forces as well as the new expectations of workers, customers, and the community that have necessitated the emergence of learning organizations.

Chapter 2 introduces the total systems learning organization model with an overview and brief synopsis of each of the five subsystems of the model: namely, learning, organization, people, knowledge, and technology. The interaction and complementarity of the subsystems are also presented.

The dimensions, principles, practices, and ideals of each of the five subsystems are explored in Chapters 3 through 7. Each chapter contains a portrait of the learning organization that best demonstrates competence and success in that subsystem. Arthur Andersen's leadership status in the subsystem of learning dynamics is highlighted in Chapter 3. Caterair International's successful organizational transformation is described in Chapter 4. Chapter 5 presents Whirlpool's worldwide efforts in empowering people to learn. In chapter 6 the knowledge management accomplishments of National Semiconductor are narrated. And in Chapter 7 the achievements of Federal Express in applying technology to organizationwide learning is reported. In the final section of each of these chapters, I have listed ten top implementation strategies for building the subsystem discussed in that chapter.

The final three chapters provide the reader with a general framework and guidelines for building a learning organization. Chapter 8 presents the 16 steps to follow in systematically moving a company into learning-organization status. Chapter 9 describes how the Rover

Group in England initiated its plan to become a learning organization and quickly became one of the outstanding learning organizations in the world. Chapter 10 addresses the conditions and strategies necessary for transforming and maintaining one's status as a learning organization.

Getting Started in Your Organization

The organization that makes learning its core value sets itself up for success. It can rapidly leverage its new knowledge into new products, new marketing strategies, and new ways of doing business.

Whether or not to become a learning organization is, therefore, no longer the question. And the question of When? should be answered with Quickly, since becoming this new species will soon be essential for surviving in the global environment. Answering the question of How? is the essence of this book. It is hoped that these pages will provide valuable guidance for you and your organization as you seek to make a quantum organizational leap into the next millennium. So let's get started. Hop into the rocket booster and launch yourself toward a starry new world of learning. Good luck!

Michael Marquardt
Reston, Virginia

Acknowledgments

Many people have been instrumental in constructing and building this book. First of all, Nancy Olson and Edward Schroer of the American Society for Training and Development, who recognized the need for a systematic, practical book on learning organizations. Many kudos also to the talented people at McGraw-Hill who edited and sculpted the final words.

I thank especially my colleagues at George Washington University and its Institute for the Study of Learning, people like David Schwandt, Chris Johnson, and Margaret Gorman, who first exposed me to the powerful benefits and theoretical complexities of organizational learning.

I am grateful for the many superb ideas and warm encouragement received from the people and organizations that already practice organizational learning: Larry Silvey, Bud Baskin, Joel Montgomery, and Michele Walker of Arthur Andersen; David Workman of Caterair International; Gil Amelio and Kevin Wheeler of National Semiconductor; Barrie Oxtoby, Bernard Sullivan, Doug Dickson and David Bower of the Rover Group; Tan Jing Hee and Chong Keng Boon of Singapore Institute of Management; Lewis Parks and Linda Morris of American Management Systems; Linda DeBerry of Federal Express; Melinda Bickerstaff of Chevy Chase Bank; and Tom Helton and Nancy Snyder of Whirlpool.

Finally, I want to thank and dedicate this book to my wife, Eveline, and children, Chris, Stephanie, Catherine, and Emily, for their love and enthusiasm in supporting this endeavor.

1
Emergence of Learning Organizations

Only by venturing into the unknown do we enable new ideas and new results to take shape.
MARGARET WHEATLEY
Leadership and the New Science

The End of the Age of Dinosaurs

Over the past 10 years, significant economic, social, and technological changes of increasing intensity have dramatically altered the environment of the business world. The large dinosaur organizations with pea-sized brains that flourished in the past cannot breathe and survive in this new atmosphere of rapid change and intense competition. The survival of the fittest is quickly becoming the survival of the *fittest-to-learn*.

Only those dinosaurs that can transform themselves into more intelligent, proficient beings will survive as we enter the next millennium. The new organization that emerges will enjoy greater knowledge, flexibility, speed, power, and learning ability to better confront the shifting needs of a new environment, more demanding customers, and smarter knowledge workers. This new species of organization will be the *learning organization* and will possess the capability to:

- Anticipate and adapt more readily to environmental impacts
- Accelerate the development of new products, processes, and services
- Become more proficient at learning from competitors and collaborators
- Expedite the transfer of knowledge from one part of the organization to another
- Learn more effectively from its mistakes
- Make greater organizational use of employees at all levels of the organization
- Shorten the time required to implement strategic changes
- Stimulate continuous improvement in all areas of the organization

Organizations that learn faster will be able to adapt quicker and thereby achieve significant strategic advantages in the global world of business. This new learning organization will be able to harness the collective genius of its people at the individual, group, and system levels; combined with improved organizational status, technology, knowledge management, and people empowerment, such companies will, according to Walter Wriston, former CEO of Citibank, "blow the competition away."

Briefly defined, learning organizations are companies that are continually transforming themselves to better manage knowledge, utilize technology, empower people, and expand learning to better adapt and succeed in the changing environment.

In this chapter, we will examine the major "winds of change" that have necessitated this species change, those forces that have changed the economic environment and the workplace, as well as both workers and customers. These changes have generated vigorous tensions that have caused organizations to reconsider their ways of thinking, managing, and operating within local, national, and international settings. In short, these are forces that have demanded either organizational adaptation or organizational extinction.

Forces Creating Need for New Species of Organization

There are four major areas which have changed profoundly over the last years of the twentieth century:

1. Economic, social and scientific environment
2. Workplace environment
3. Customers
4. Workers

Changing Economic, Social, and Scientific Environment

Several conditions and factors have altered the world in which we live today and the world in which we work:

- Globalization
- Economic and marketing competition
- Environmental and ecological pressures
- New sciences of quantum physics and chaos theory
- Knowledge era
- Societal turbulence

Let's briefly explore each of these forces and reflect on how they have created a world in which only learning organizations will be able to survive and succeed.

Globalization.   Today more and more companies—McDonald's, Xerox, Motorola, Honda, Samsung, among thousands of others—are manufacturing and selling chiefly outside their country of origin. This is so common that we hardly know if a company is French, Japanese, Swedish, or American. Coca Cola earns more money in Japan than in the United States. Over 70 percent of profits for the $20 billion U.S. music industry are from outside our country. More than 70 percent of the employees of Canon work outside Japan. Over 100,000 U.S. firms are engaged in global ventures valued at over $1 trillion. Ten percent of U.S. manufacturing is foreign-owned and employs over three million Americans.

Globalization represents the converging of economic and social forces, values, and opportunities. Pundits have called globalization the root cause for change in the 1990s and beyond.

Travel, trade, and television have laid the groundwork for a more collective experience of employees everywhere. More and more workers around the world share common tastes in foods (hamburgers, pizza, tacos), fashion (denim jeans), and fun (Disney, rock music, television). People are watching the same movies, reading the same magazines, and dancing the same dances from Boston to Bangkok to Buenos

Aires. Ever more of us speak a common language—English, which is now spoken by more than a billion people in over 100 countries, where it is either the first or second language. The English language, which like all other languages carries culture and social values, has become the global language of media, computers, and business.

Economically, a single global marketplace has been created by five factors: abundant energy sources, competitiveness of global corporations, global telecommunications (enhanced by fiber-optics, satellites, and computer technology), growing free trade among nations, and worldwide accessible financial services.

A number of incentives have encouraged organizations to globalize including:

- Ability to earn additional income on existing technology
- Access to foreign technology, skills, knowledge, capital, and human and natural resources
- Increased global customer base
- Increased potential to offset lack of demand for seasonal products
- Increased product service life cycle
- Lowered transportation costs and time
- Opportunities for larger profits due to economies of scale in production, logistics, and marketing
- Opportunities to gain an edge in reputation and credibility

Each of these incentives will continue to grow and increase the rapidity with which companies are compelled to move beyond domestic markets. Organizations will have no choice but to shop the world for human resources, technology, markets, and business partners.

Certain industries have globalized earlier than others, especially telecommunication, electronics and computers, finance and banking, transportation, automotive, pharmaceutical, petroleum, and biotechnology. Even the largest companies in the biggest national markets are not able to survive on their home markets alone. Thinking and operating globally has become pivotal for organizational survival and growth in the twenty-first century.

Economic and Marketing Competition. Globalization, with its huge economic and marketing repercussions, has generated huge competitive pressures on all corporations. Twenty-five percent of the Fortune 500 companies disappear every 10 years. Markets are rapidly changing. Consumers are pushing for new performance standards in quality, variety, customization, convenience, time, and innovation. These new demands for quality, the constant change of taste, the existence of global fads, and short product life cycles are forcing new global partnerships and alliances.

Regional trade agreements are beginning to emerge. In 1992, with the creation of the European Common Market, Western Europe became the world's largest market with more than 350 million people and a GNP of over $10 trillion, 43 percent of the world's total. A single currency is scheduled to be introduced and the free movement of labor, goods, services, and capital has begun. The North American Free Trade Agreement (NAFTA) brings together the economic might of the United States, Canada, and Mexico. Other regional trade agreements are being pursued or are already in place in Asia, Latin America, Africa, and in the Middle East.

Environmental and Ecological Pressures. Industrial and population growth has created tremendous environmental problems throughout the world. The city of Karachi provides only 30 percent of the water it needs, forcing the poor to drink untreated water, which has led to epidemics and deaths. The pollution in industrial countries will cause as much as 50 percent of their populations to suffer from a rash or some other skin disease each year (compared to 2 percent in the 1950s). At the present discard rate, Tokyo will run out of dump sites within two years. Tokyo's dumps are already threatening the fishing and shipping industries (*Time*, January 11, 1993, p. 36).

Fortune magazine has declared that environmental and ecological concerns are "not only the biggest business issue of the 1990's, but a mainstream movement of massive worldwide force. Companies must and are moving toward eco-responsibility" (February 12, 1992).

Today, people believe that if corporations do not move quickly, we may not be able to avert environmental damage so severe that future generations will be unable to meet basic requirements for food, energy, and clean, healthy air. A recent survey of global executives by Booz, Allen, and Hamilton revealed the increased awareness of the responsibility of corporations in maintaining, instead of destroying, the environment. Managers and employees are being encouraged to find ways for their organization to be ever mindful of being energy efficient in production and services. Corporations are being forced to search for environmentally advantaged technologies.

The New Sciences of Quantum Physics and Chaos Theory.
Newtonian physics is a science of quantifiable determinism, of clear cause and effect, of linear thinking and controllable futures. It believes that a result occurs when one factor impacts on another. In a Newtonian

mindset, people engage in complex planning for a world that they believe is predictable. They continually search for better methods of objectively perceiving the world, a mindset that, according to Margaret Wheatley (*Leadership and the New Science*), is "unempowering and disabling to all of us."

Although the field of quantum physics was developed by scientists in the early part of the twentieth century, few organizations or managers are aware of, much less using this new science.

Quantum physics deals with the world at the subatomic level, of the implicate patterns out of which seemingly discrete events arise. It is knowledgeable of the vast empty spaces which are filled with fields that are the basic substance of the universe. In the quantum world relationship is the key determiner of what is observed and how particles manifest themselves. The observer cannot observe anything without interfering or, more importantly, participating in its creation. The quantum universe is enacted in an environment rich in relationships, in a world of process and not just of things. Quantum physics has made scientists aware of waves and holograms, one which goes from the predictable to the surprising.

People with an understanding of quantum physics realize that one cannot predict with absolute certainty, that chaos is a part of the reality. The new science causes one to change the ways he or she understands, designs, leads, and manages organizations. It helps leaders to better deal with order and change, autonomy and control, structure and flexibility, planning and innovation.

The Knowledge Era.   According to leading futurists and business leaders, we have clearly entered the *knowledge era*; the new economy is a *knowledge economy*. Knowledge provides the key raw material for wealth creation and is the fountain of organizational and personal power.

Information is created continuously in every corner of the globe, and doubles every three to four years. Brainpower is becoming a company's most valuable asset. Thomas Stewart, in a recent issue of *Fortune* magazine, asserts that "Brainpower...has never before been so important for business. Every company depends increasingly on knowledge—patents, process, management skills, technologies, information about customers and suppliers, and old-fashioned experience....This knowledge that exists in an organization can be used to create differential advantage. In other words, it's the sum of everything everybody in your company knows that gives you a competitive edge in the marketplace."

In most companies the management of intellectual capital is still uncharted territory. Few executives understand how to navigate it.

Managing know-how is not like managing cash or buildings, yet intellectual investments need to be treated every bit as painstakingly.

The first step in getting more from your intellectual assets, according to Stewart, is to find them. Often, companies are startled to learn how much intellectual capital they have. Step two is matching the company's intellectual needs with its strategic plan. Once you have a handle on the intellectual assets, the company must learn how to best package them.

The greatest challenge for the manager of intellectual capital is to create an organization that can redistribute its knowledge. Intellectual capital is useless, unless it moves. By finding ways to make knowledge move, an organization can create a value network—not just a value chain.

Simply put, knowledge has become more important for organizations than financial resources, market position, technology, or any other company asset. Knowledge is seen as the main resource used in performing work in an organization. The organization's traditions, culture, technology, operations, systems, and procedures are all based on knowledge and expertise.

Knowledge is needed to increase the abilities of employees to improve products and services—thereby providing quality service to clients and consumers. Expertise is necessary to update products and services, change systems and structures, and communicate solutions to problems. In the new knowledge economy, individuals at every level and in all kinds of companies will be challenged to develop new knowledge, to take responsibility for their new ideas, and to pursue them as far as they can go. The job of the manager will be to create an environment that allows workers to increase knowledge.

Walter Wriston, in *The Twilight of Sovereignty: How the Information Revolution is Transforming the World*, writes that, ultimately, the location of the new economy is not in technology, be it a microchip or a global communications network, but in the human mind.

Robert Reich, U.S. Secretary of Labor and author of *The Work of Nations*, points out that "corporations no longer focus on products as such; their business strategies increasingly center upon specialized knowledge" (p. 8).

In the successful organizations of the future (those offering high value), only one asset grows more valuable as it is used—the knowledge skills of people. Unlike machinery that gradually wears out, materials that become depleted, patents and copyrights that grow obsolete, and trademarks that lose their ability to comfort, the knowledge and insights that come from the learning of employees actually increase in value when used and practiced.

Societal Turbulence.   Massive societal changes are taking place throughout the globe. Eastern Europe has overthrown the yoke of Communism and is now in the midst of further divisions with ethnic warfare. Japan, an economic powerhouse, is undergoing profound economic challenges. China, India, and much of Africa are moving from planned state-run economies to a more capitalistic, free-enterprise status. Massive migrations continue in every continent. The specter of AIDS is affecting the availability of an educated, professional workforce in central Africa. It also impacts the health costs and even relationships and social interactions around the world. In the United States, the highly explosive issues of abortion and gay rights are dividing people of every religious and political persuasion. Society is becoming ever more urban. By the year 2000, more than 50 percent of all people will live in cities; there will be 21 megacities of more than 10 million inhabitants. In most of these cities poverty, chaos, and danger will be the daily staple of life.

Changing Workplace Environment

Five forces have recently and quickly transformed the workplace:

- Information technology and the informated organization
- Organization structure and size
- Total quality management movement
- Workforce diversity and mobility
- Boom in temporary help

Information Technology and the Informated Organization.   Alvin Toffler writes how the advanced global economy cannot run for 30 seconds without the information technology of computers and other new and rapidly improving complexities of production. Yet, today's best computers and CAD/CAM systems will be Stone Age primitives within a few years.

We have indeed entered an era of ever-increasing technological advancement—with new technologies such as optoelectronics, cyberspace, information highways, digital video, informating, local area networks, groupware, virtual reality, and electronic classrooms. The power of computer technology has progressed from mainframe to desktop to briefcase portable to user's hand. More and more of a company's operations are being totally automated. The impact on organizational work and on learning has been overwhelming.

Organizations have also become more and more "informated," that is, able to immediately acquire information that can be used to get a job done, generate new information as a by-product, and develop new information. An example of informating is the grocery store's use of data from the checkout counter.

The new, informated organization has become a place where the expansion of knowledge becomes very important. Learning is no longer a separate activity that occurs either before one enters the workplace or in remote classroom settings. Nor is it an activity reserved for a managerial group. According to Shoshana Zuboff, the author of *In The Age of the Smart Machine*, the behaviors that define learning and those that define being productive "are one and the same. Learning is the heart of productive activity. To put it simply, learning is the new form of labor" (p. 395).

Organization Structure and Size. As more companies realize that the key resource of business is not capital, personnel, or facilities, but rather knowledge, information, and ideas, many new ways of viewing the organization begin to emerge. Everywhere companies are restructuring, creating integrated organizations, global networks, and leaner corporate centers. Organizations are becoming more fluid, ever shifting in size, shape, and arrangements.

Many of these changes, in one form or another, have led to the path of *federalism* as the way to manage increasingly complex organizations in the increasingly rapidly changing environment. In *The Age of Reason* Charles Handy attributes the popularity and success of this way of structuring and sizing organizations to the fact that federalism is an effective way of dealing with six paradoxes: (1) power and control, (2) being both big and small at the same time, (3) being autonomous but within bounds, (4) encouraging variety but within a shared purpose, (5) individuality but also partnership, and (6) global and yet local.

Many businesses have moved in the direction of federalism for several reasons:

- Its autonomy releases energy.
- It allows people to be well-informed.
- Its units are bound together by trust and a common goal and not forced control.
- Power is delegated to the lowest possible point in the organization (a good example of this is Motorola employees who were told by the former Chairman Robert Galvin that they have all the authority of the Chairman when they are with customers).
- The decentralized structure and interdependence spreads power around and thereby avoids the risks of a central bureaucracy.
- It is very flexible and can never be static.

- Authority must be earned from those over whom it is exercised.
- People have the right and duty to be responsible and recognized for their work.
- Organizations are much flatter (have little hierarchy) without losing efficiency.

Another form of restructuring that is rapidly gaining popularity is that of virtual organizations. A *virtual organization* is a temporary network of independent companies, suppliers, customers, and even rivals linked by information technology to share skills, costs, and access to one another's markets. In its purest form, a company decides to focus on the thing it does best. Then it links with other companies, each bringing to the combination its own special ability. It will mix and match what it does best with the best of the other companies. For example, a manufacturer will manufacture while relying on a product-design outfit to sell the output.

Such a "best of everything" organization could be a world-class competitor, with the speed, the muscle and the leading-edge technology to pounce on the briefest of opportunities. The February 8, 1993, issue of *Business Week* states that the virtual model "could become the most important organizational innovation since the 1920's" or when Pierre DuPont and Alfred Sloan developed the principle of decentralization to organize giant complex corporations.

The virtual corporation will have neither central office nor organization chart, and no hierarchy or vertical integration. Teams of people in different companies will routinely work together. After the business is done, the virtual organization disbands.

Charles Savage of Digital sees the emergence of these network-type organizations replacing the more traditional bureaucratic structure with the organizational shifts shown in Figure 1-1.

Three other emerging management theories affecting organizational structure and gaining popularity in the marketplace are:

Reengineering. Reengineering is a fundamental rethinking and redesign of business systems which urges an overhaul of job designs, organization structures and management systems. Work should be organized around outcomes, not tasks or functions.

Core competencies. Companies organize around what they do best. Therefore, they structure according to competencies instead of according to product or market.

Organizational architecture. This is a structural form that evolves around autonomous work teams and strategic alliances.

Total Quality Management Movement.   The ability to attract and retain customers by meeting their needs with quality products and quality service has become a pivotal issue for all organizations. In a global economy, quality standards are not set in the boardroom, but in the worldwide marketplace. Customers now have many choices, and quality is of high importance. Most organizations have established Total Quality Management (TQM) programs. Every year more U.S. companies zealously seek the Malcolm Baldrige National Quality Award. Annual Quality Conferences are attended by thousands of business leaders. Corporations relate continuous improvement in manufacturing and service to continued success. Competitive advantage comes from the continuous, incremental innovation and refinement of a variety of ideas that spread throughout the organization.

Workplace Diversity and Mobility.   The global workforce is becoming ever more diverse and mobile. Hispanics and Asians will represent over 25 percent of the total U.S. workforce by the year 2000. Already, in California, Texas and Florida, nearly half the workforce is Black, Hispanic or Asian.

Physicists at Bell Laboratories are as likely to come from universities in England or India as from Princeton or MIT. At research centers around the world, the first language of the biochemists is as likely to be Hindi, Japanese, or German as it is English or French. It is routine for U.S. hospitals to advertise in Dublin and Manila for nurses.

Corporations are increasingly reaching across borders to find the skills they need. These movements of workers are driven by the

Dimension	Bureaucratic	Network
Critical tasks	Physical	Mental
Relationships	Hierarchical	Peer to peer
Levels	Many	Few
Structures	Functional	Multidisciplinary teams
Boundaries	Fixed	Permeable
Competitive thrust	Vertical integration	Outsourcing and alliances
Management style	Autocratic	Participative
Culture	Compliance and tradition	Commitment and results
People	Homogeneous	Diverse
Strategic focus	Efficiency	Innovation

Figure 1-1. Organizational shifts.

growing gap between the world's supplies and demands for them. Much of the planet's skilled and unskilled human resources are being produced in the developing world. Yet, most of the well-paid, high skilled jobs are being generated in the cities of the industrialized world.

William Johnston, who recently completed an exhaustive study of global work patterns, identified four major implications of the mobile, culturally diverse workforce on global corporations:

Relocation. A massive relocation of people, especially young and better-educated, will flock to urban areas around the world.

Competition for labor. More industrialized nations will come to rely on, and even compete for, foreign born workers.

Improved productivity. Labor-short, immigrant-poor countries like Japan and Sweden will be compelled to improve labor productivity dramatically to avoid slow economic growth. The need for increased outsourcing of jobs to other countries is escalating.

Standardization. There is a gradual standardization of labor practices around the world in areas of vacation time, workplace safety, and employee rights.

Johnston adds that nations that have slow-growing work forces but rapid growth in service-sector jobs (Japan, United States, Germany) will become magnets for immigrants. Nations whose educational systems produce prospective workers faster than their economies can absorb them (Argentina, Egypt, Philippines, Poland, Russia) will export people.

The combination of a globalized workforce with massive mobility forces organizations to be able to work with growing numbers of people with differing cultures, customs, values, beliefs, and practices.

Boom in Temporary Workforce.   Even as the job market in the United States has recovered and unemployment is under 6 percent, more and more companies are depending heavily on temporary help. Temp outfits have added more than 1 million workers over the past three years, and their employment is rising at 17 percent annually. Organizations in the telecommunications, computers, heaving manufacturing and banking fields are the greatest users of temp help.

Businesses have made temp help an integral part of the hiring process as well as overall human resources policy. The hiring of temporary workers allows for greater flexibility for organizations, but at the expense of worker loyalty and knowledge retention.

Changing Customer Expectations

Global competition has offered customers a more varied and higher quality of choices. They are now able to choose the products and services they want based on the best:

Cost. What is the least expensive, most economical

Quality. No defects; meeting and exceeding the customer's expectations

Time. Available as quickly as possible

Service. Pleasant, courteous, available and on products which are reparable or replaceable

Innovation. New, something not yet envisioned by the customer when produced (e.g., Sony walkman)

Customization. Tailored to very specific needs

Changing Employee Expectations

The final area which has undergone significant changes in the past several years relates to the expectations of today's worker. Organizations must more than ever respond to the employee's new job skills, new job roles, and new job expectations.

New Job Skills. As society moves from the industrial era to the knowledge era, job requirements are changing. We are moving from the age of manufacturing to an era of mentofacturing; i.e., where the production is more with the mind (mento) than with the hands (manu). Employees are moving from needing repetitive skills to knowing how to deal with surprises and exceptions, from depending on memory and facts to being spontaneous and creative, from risk avoidance to risk taking, from focusing on policies and procedures to building collaboration with people.

A U.S. Department of Labor report, *Economic Change and the American Workforce*, notes: "The competitive workplace today regardless of the product or service is a high-skill environment designed around technology and people who are technically competent. Assembly line workers must now understand their work as part of a much larger whole." As mid-level jobs disappear, U.S. society is dividing between high earners, "empowered" in the workforce because of their high level of skills, and those in survival wage jobs, consigned to unskilled employment or unemployment.

Workers who thrive will have the three skills essential in driving the emerging businesses:

- Problem identifier skills (required to help customers understand their needs and how those needs can best be met by customized products)
- Problem solving skills (required to put things together in unique ways)
- Strategic broker skills (needed to link problem-solvers and problem identifiers)

According to Robert Reich, U.S. Secretary of Labor, enterprises requiring high knowledge skills will derive profits not from scale and volume, but from the following four aspects:

- Continuous discovery of new linkages between solutions and needs
- Specialized research, engineering, and design services necessary to solve problems
- Specialized sales, marketing and consulting services necessary to identify problems
- Specialized strategic, financial and management services for brokering the first two

New Job Roles.   We are now in the era of knowledge workers. By the beginning of the next century, three quarters of the jobs in the U.S. economy will involve creating and processing knowledge. Knowledge workers have already discovered that continual learning is not only a prerequisite of employment but is a major form of work.

Peter Drucker sees organizations composed more and more of *knowledge workers*. Not only senior executives, but employees at all levels must be highly educated, highly skilled knowledge workers. In the new post-capitalist society, knowledge is not just another resource alongside the traditional factors of production, land, labor and capital. It is the only meaningful resource in today's workforce. In an economy based on knowledge, the knowledge worker is the single greatest asset.

Corporations can no longer focus only on products as such; their business increasingly depends on the specialized knowledge, the know-how, of their employees. These knowledge employees are rapidly becoming the most valuable asset of corporations; they are the critical core of the company, the essence of the business from which all revenues flow. And unlike other assets of the company which lose value over time, the know-how of employees actually increase in value when used and practiced.

New Worker Expectations. A fascinating aspect about knowledge workers is that they do, in fact, own the means of production and they can take it out of the door with them at any moment. Therefore, managers have to attract and motivate; reward, recognize, and retain; train, educate, and improve; and, in the most remarkable reversal of all, serve and satisfy knowledge workers.

Our most valuable and valued workers today want the opportunity to be challenged, to solve difficult problems. They want freedom to explore, to take risks, to be innovative and creative. They desire flexibility, responsibility and accountability. They want to work with managers who empower them, who respect them, who can mentor them to new heights.

Organizations must provide a structure in which knowledge workers can apply their knowledge. Specifically, organizations must expedite contact with other knowledge workers, since it is through dialogue and interaction with other knowledge workers that they can refine and improve their ideas, and thereby help the firm even more.

Emergence of Learning Organizations

Albert Einstein once wrote that "No problem can be solved from the same consciousness that created it; we must learn to see the world anew." The changes in the four areas of environment, workplace, customer and worker have altered the world of work so dramatically that old "dinosaur-like" organizations are no longer able to respond to these changes, to handle these new challenges. As Einstein had forewarned, these new problems won't be able to be solved using the same structures, mindsets or knowledge that had worked for organizations in the past.

Today, there are a growing number of organizational people who are becoming increasing aware that the knowledge, the strategies, the leadership, and the technology of yesterday will not lead to success in tomorrow's world. It has become obvious to them that companies have to increase their corporate capacity to learn if they are to function successfully in an environment that includes continual mergers, rapid technological changes, massive societal change, and increasing competition.

With all these challenges and potential benefits to the organization, it was just a matter of time before the new species of learning organizations would arrive.

To obtain and sustain competitive advantage in this new world, companies realized that they would have to evolve into a higher form of learning capability, to be able to learn better and faster from their successes and failures, from within and from outside. They would need to continuously transform themselves into an organization where everyone, groups and individuals, would quantumly increase their adaptive and productive capabilities. Only if they increased their capacity to learn would they be able to avoid the fate of the dinosaur, which had not been able to adapt to the changing environment.

In the early 1990s, a number of organizations have started up the ladder of becoming a learning organization. Companies such as General Electric, Corning, Federal Express, Ford, Motorola, and Pacific Bell in the United States; Sheerness Steel, Rover, and ABB in Europe, and Singapore Airlines and Samsung in Asia are among the early and more successful pioneers.

As is the case of many evolutionary processes, some of the other organizations than began the process of adaptation and learning did not acquire enough transmutation to sustain long-lasting change. They were not fully prepared to give up the security of their present size and successes, to fully and systematically metamorphose into the new species of a learning organization. They chose to take on smaller, safer chunks of change; more modest changes such as quality circles or reeingineering where only a portion of the full benefits of organizational learning could be realized.

Enabling Forces to Build Learning Organizations

Fortunately, some of the same forces that created the changes in the environment and atmosphere can serve as the foundation stones for building the learning organization.

For example, the competitive and technological forces that have mandated a flatter, seamless organization enable that company to move knowledge more quickly with less internal filtering. Know-how workers who have greater mobility and choices force an organization to empower these workers so they can be more productive. Customer expectations and options require companies to continually learn new ways to "delight" them. The power of the computer and telecommunications erases distances and time as well as facilitates information flow. Rapid and ongoing changes in the skill needs of workers have forced them to be continuous learners who do not have the luxury of "waiting to be trained."

The organization which is able to capture all of these forces and systematically synergize them will be the one able to make quantum leaps up the evolutionary ladder to the next stage of organizational life - the learning organization.

Experience and research have shown that when companies incorporate 5 distinct subsystems into the learning organization process, i.e., learning, organization, people, knowledge and technology, they are quicker and much more successful in becoming a learning organization. Attempting to become a learning company without all five of these dimensions will be insufficient and frustrating. Full throttle on all gears is necessary to go from a nonlearning to a learning organization.

The next chapters will carefully explore each of the subsystems and how they interface and complement one another. The core of the learning organization, of course, is the learning subsystem—at the individual, group, and organizational levels. This subsystem will be presented in Chapter 3. Each of the other subsystems—organization, people, knowledge and technology—that are necessary to effect and enhance the quality and impact of the learning are examined in Chapters 4 to 7.

In Chapter 2 we will graphically present the total Systems Learning Organization model, and show how each of the subsystems support and energize one another. Let's begin climbing.

2
The Systems-Linked Organization Model

A learning organization, systematically defined, is an organization which learns powerfully and collectively and is continually transforming itself to better collect, manage, and use knowledge for corporate success. It empowers people within and outside the company to learn as they work. Technology is utilized to optimize both learning and productivity.

It is important to note the difference between the terms *learning organization* and *organizational learning*. In discussing learning organizations, we are focusing on the *what*, and describing the systems, principles, and characteristic of organizations that learn and produce as a collective entity. Organizational learning, on the other hand, refers to *how* organizational learning occurs, i.e., the skills and processes of building and utilizing knowledge. Organizational learning as such is just one dimension or element of a learning organization.

There are a number of important dimensions and characteristics of a learning organization:

- Learning is accomplished by the organizational system as a whole, almost as if the organization were a single brain.

- Organizational members recognize the critical importance of ongoing organizationwide learning for the organization's current as well as future success.

- Learning is a continuous, strategically used process—integrated with and running parallel to work.
- There is a focus on creativity and generative learning.
- Systems thinking is fundamental.
- People have continuous access to information and data resources that are important to the company's success.
- A corporate climate exists that encourages, rewards, and accelerates individual and group learning.
- Workers network in an innovative, communitylike manner inside and outside the organization.
- Change is embraced, and unexpected surprises and even failures are viewed as opportunities to learn.
- It is agile and flexible.
- Everyone is driven by a desire for quality and continuous improvement.
- Activities are characterized by aspiration, reflection, and conceptualization.
- There are well-developed core competencies that serve as a taking-off point for new products and services.
- It possesses the ability to continuously adapt, renew, and revitalize itself in response to the changing environment.

These characteristics are part of the systems-linked learning organization model which is made up of five closely interrelated subsystems that interface and support one another (see Figure 2-1).

The core subsystem of the learning organization is learning and this dimension permeates the other four subsystems. Learning takes place at the individual, group, and organizational levels. The skills (or disciplines as Peter Senge refers to them) of systems thinking, mental model, personal mastery, team learning, shared vision, and dialogue are necessary to maximize organizational learning.

Each of the other subsystems—organization, people, knowledge, and technology—are necessary to enhance and augment the quality and impact of the learning. They are indispensable partners for building, maintaining, and sustaining learning and productivity in the learning organization. The five subsystems are dynamically interrelated and complement each other. If any subsystem is weak or absent, the effectiveness of the other subsystems is significantly weakened.

In this chapter we will introduce the subsystems of learning, organization, people, knowledge, and technology. In chapters 3 to 7, we will

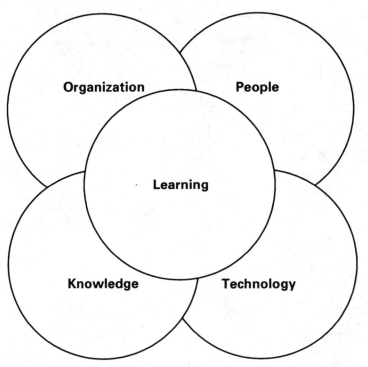

Figure 2-1. Systems learning organization model.

present and explore in depth the concepts, principles, strategies, and corporate leaders of each of these five subsystems.

Learning Subsystem

The learning subsystem refers to levels of learning, types of learning crucial for organizational learning, and critical organizational learning skills (Figure 2-2).

Levels of Learning

There are three levels of learning present in learning organizations:

Individual learning refers to the change of skills, insights, knowledge, attitudes, and values acquired by a person through self-study, technology-based instruction, insight, and observation.

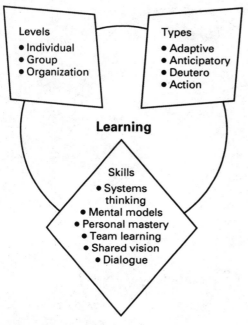

Figure 2-2. Learning subsystem.

Group or team learning alludes to the increase in knowledge, skills, and competency which is accomplished by and within groups.

Organization learning represents the enhanced intellectual and productive capability gained through corporatewide commitment and opportunity for continuous improvement. It differs from individual and group/team learning in two basic respects. First, organizational learning occurs through the shared insights, knowledge, and mental models of members of the organization. Second, organizational learning builds on past knowledge and experience—that is, on organizational memory which depends on institutional mechanisms (e.g., policies, strategies, and explicit models) used to retain knowledge.

Types of Learning

There are several types or ways of learning that are of significance and value to the learning organization. Although each type is distinctive, there is often overlap and complementarity of the various types. Therefore, a particular learning occurrence may be identified as being of more than one type. For example, action learning may be further classified as being adaptive or anticipatory.

Adaptive, anticipatory, and generative learning are defined as follows: Adaptive learning is learning from experience and reflection. Anticipatory learning is the process of acquiring knowledge from expecting the future (a vision-action-reflection approach), whereas generative learning is the learning that is created from reflection, analysis, or creativity.

Single-loop, double-loop, and deutero learning are differentiated by the degree of reflection placed on action that has occurred in the organization.

Action learning/action reflection learning involves reflecting on real problems using the formula of *L* (learning) = *P* (existing or programmed knowledge) + *Q* (questioning insight).

Skills (Disciplines) of Organizational Learning

There are six key skills (or disciplines, as Peter Senge refers to them) needed to initiate and maximize organizational learning:

Systems thinking represents a conceptual framework one uses to make full patterns clearer, and to help one see how to change them effectively

Mental models are the deeply ingrained assumptions that influence how we understand the world and how we take action. For example, our mental model or image of learning or work or patriotism impacts how we relate and act in situations where those concepts are operating.

Personal mastery indicates the high level of proficiency in a subject or skill area. It requires a commitment to lifelong learning so as to develop an expertise or special, enjoyed proficiency in whatever one does in the organization.

Team learning (the skill, not the level as described above) focuses on the process of aligning and developing the capacity of a team to create the learning and results its members truly desire.

Shared vision involves the skill of unearthing shared pictures of the future that foster genuine commitment and enrollment rather than compliance.

Dialogue denotes the high level of listening and communication between people. It requires the free and creative exploration of subtle issues, a deep listening to one another, and suspension of one's own views. The discipline of dialogue involves learning how to recognize the patterns of interaction in teams that promote or undermine learning. For example, the patterns of defensiveness are often deeply ingrained in how a group of people or an organization operates. If unrecognized or avoided, they undermine learning. If recognized and surfaced creatively, they can actually accelerate learning. Dialogue is the critical medium for connecting, inventing, and coordinating learning and action in the workplace.

Organization Subsystem

The second subsystem of a learning organization is the organization itself, the setting and body in which the learning occurs. The four key dimensions or components of this subsystem are vision, culture, strategy, and structure (see Figure 2-3).

Culture refers to the values, beliefs, practices, rituals, and customs of an organization. It helps to shape behavior and fashion perceptions. In a learning organization, the corporate culture is one in which learning is recognized as absolutely critical for business success, where learning has become a habit and an integrated part of all organizational functions. This rich adaptable culture creates integrated relationships and enhances learning by encouraging values such as teamwork, self-management, empowerment, and sharing. It is the opposite of a closed, rigid, bureaucratic architecture.

Vision captures a company's hopes, goals, and direction for the future. It is the image of the organization that is transmitted inside

Figure 2-3. Organization subsystem.

and outside the organization. In a learning organization it depicts and portrays the desired future picture of the company in which learning and learners create the company's continuously new and improving products and services.

Strategy relates to the action plans, methodologies, tactics, and steps that are employed to reach a company's vision and goals. In a learning organization, these are strategies that optimize the learning acquired, transferred, and utilized in all company actions and operations.

Structure includes the departments, levels, and configurations of the company. A learning organization is a streamlined, flat, boundaryless structure that maximizes contact, information flow, local responsibility, and collaboration within and outside the organization.

People Subsystem

The people subsystem of the learning organization includes employees, managers/leaders, customers, business partners (suppliers, vendors, and subcontractors), and the community itself (Figure 2-4). Each of these groups is valuable to the learning organization, and all need to be empowered and enabled to learn.

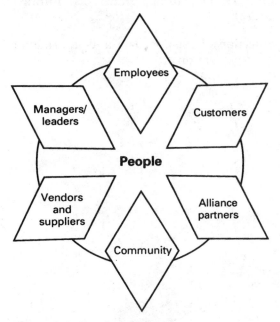

Figure 2-4. People subsystem.

Employees as learners are empowered and expected to learn, to plan for their future competencies, to take action and risks, and to solve problems.

Managers/leaders as learners carry out coaching, mentoring, and modeling roles with a primary responsibility of generating and enhancing learning opportunities for the people around them.

Customers as learners participate in identifying needs, receiving training, and being linked to the learning of the organization.

Suppliers and vendors as learners can receive and contribute to instructional programs.

Alliance partners as learners can benefit by sharing competencies and knowledge.

Community groups as learners include social, educational, and economic agencies who can share in the providing and receiving of learning.

Knowledge Subsystem

The knowledge subsystem of a learning organization refers to the management of acquired and generated knowledge of the organization. It includes the acquisition, creation, storage, transfer, and utilization of knowledge (see Figure 2-5).

Acquisition refers to the collection of existing data and information from within and outside the organization.

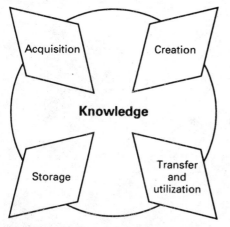

Figure 2-5. Knowledge subsystem.

Creation involves new knowledge that is created within the organization through problem solving and insights.

Storage is the coding and preserving of the organization's valued knowledge for easy access by any staff member, at any time, and from anywhere.

Transfer and utilization includes the mechanical, electronic, and interpersonal movement of information and knowledge, both intentionally and unintentionally, throughout the organization as well as its application and use by members of the organization.

The knowledge elements of organizational learning are ongoing and interactive instead of sequential and independent. The collection and distribution of information occurs through multiple channels, each having different time frames. An example is an on-line newsletter which systematically gathers, organizes, and disseminates the collective knowledge of the organization's members.

Technology Subsystem

The technology subsystem is the supporting, integrated technological networks and information tools that allow access to and exchange of information and learning. It includes technical processes, systems, and structure for collaboration, coaching, coordination, and other knowl-

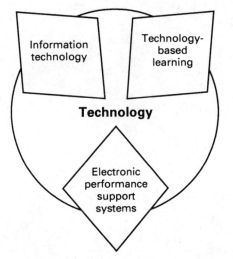

Figure 2-6. Technology subsystem.

edge skills. It encompasses electronic tools and advanced methods for learning, such as computer conferencing, simulation, and computer-supported collaboration. All these tools work to create knowledge freeways.

The three major components of the technology subsystem are information technology, technology-based learning, and electronic performance support systems (see Figure 2-6).

Information technology refers to the computer-based technology that gathers, codes, stores, and transfers information across organizations and across the world.

Technology-based learning involves the utilization of video, audio, and computer-based multimedia training for the purpose of delivering and sharing knowledge and skills.

Electronic performance support systems (EPSS) use data (text, visual, or audio) and knowledge bases to capture, store, and distribute information throughout the organization so as to help workers reach their highest level of performance in the fastest possible time, with the least personnel support. EPSS consist of several components including, but not limited to, interactive training, productivity and application software, and expert and feedback systems

In chapters 3 through 7, we will examine in much greater detail the dimensions, principles, strategies, and corporate exemplars of each of the five subsystems that form the systems-linked learning organization model to build a sturdy, firm structure that will ensure global learning and success. Let the construction and building of our learning organization begin.

3

Building Dynamic Learning Throughout the Organization

Learning is the new form of labor.
SHOSHANA ZUBOFF

The core subsystem of the learning organization model is the learning itself. The speed, quality, and leverage of the learning processes and content form the foundation and nutrient which supports, nourishes, and flows through the other subsystems of the learning organization.

The learning subsystem (Figure 3-1) is composed of three complementary dimensions: (1) levels of learning (individual, group, and organizational); (2) types of learning (adaptive, anticipatory, deutero, single and double loop, and action-reflection); and (3) skills (systems thinking, mental models, personal mastery, team learning, shared vision, and dialogue).

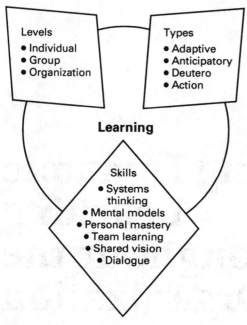

Figure 3-1. Learning subsystem.

Learning in Organizational Settings

Before examining each of these three dimensions of the learning subsystem, it is important that one understands and appreciates some basic principles of learning itself, particularly as they relate to the organizational context.

Learning has traditionally been defined as a process by which individuals gain new knowledge and insights that result in a change of behavior and actions. It comprises the cognitive (intellectual), affective (emotional), and psychomotor (physical) domains.

Edgar Schein, professor at Harvard, has written numerous books on individual and organizational learning. He points out that for individuals or organizations to learn competently, they should first understand that there are distinctly different kinds of learning which have very different time horizons associated with them and which may be applicable at different stages of a learning or change process. He cites three kinds of learning:

1. *Habit and skill learning.*   This kind of learning is slow because it calls for practice and the willingness of the learner to be temporari-

ly incompetent. For this type of learning to take hold, we need opportunities to practice, opportunities to make errors, and consistent rewards for correct responses.

2. *Emotional conditioning and learned anxiety.* This kind of learning is the most potent. As in the conditioning of Pavlov's dog, once this type of learning has occurred, it will continue long after original causes have been discontinued.

3. *Knowledge acquisition.* Most learning theories imply that the essence of learning is the acquiring of information and knowledge through various kinds of cognitive activities. This point of view, according to Schein, ignores three things:

- That learning can only happen if the learner recognizes a problem and is motivated to learn.
- Even with insight, the learner often cannot produce the right type of behavior or skill consistently to solve the problem.
- Insight does not automatically change behavior, and until behavior has changed and new results have been observed, we do not know whether what we are learning cognitively is valid or not.

Peter Senge, in *The Fifth Discipline*, p. 191, agrees that "learning has very little to do with taking in information. Learning, instead, is a process that is about enhancing capacity. Learning is about building the capability to create that which you previously couldn't create. It's ultimately related to action, which information is not."

Learning, ultimately, is a social phenomenon—our ability to learn and what we can know is determined by the quality and openness of our relationships. Our mental models of the world and of ourselves grow out of our relationships with others. Dialogue with others, which involves continuous critical reappraisal of our views, increases the possibilities for learning. Learning and dialogue are incompatible with self-sufficiency.

It is important to recognize that learning is not equally valuable or applicable; some things that are learned are dysfunctional, and some insights or skills that would lead to useful new actions are often hard to come by in a given organization.

The New Learning

Learning in today's organizational settings has become, for many, a new form of learning. This new learning contains several specific characteristics:

1. It is performance-based (i.e., tied to business objectives).

2. Importance is placed on learning processes (learning how to learn) as much if not more than on the learning content.

3. The ability to define learning needs is as important as the answers.

4. Organizationwide opportunities are created to develop knowledge, skills, and attitudes.

5. Learning is, in part, a product of the activity, context, and culture in which it is developed and used.

6. People are more willing and able to learn that which they have helped create.

7. A critical survival skill is the ability to know what one must know and to learn on one's own.

8. Continuous learning is essential for survival and success in today's world.

9. Facilitators can accelerate learning by helping people think critically.

10. Learning should accommodate and challenge different learning style preferences.

11. Learning is part of work, a part of everybody's job description.

12. Learning involves a cyclical, iterative process of planning, implementing, and reflecting on action.

Levels of Learning

Learning in organizations can occur at three levels—individual, group/team, and organization. Learning organizations have developed the capacity of encouraging and maximizing all three levels.

Individual Learning

Individual learning is needed for organizational learning since individuals form the units of groups and organizations. Peter Senge asserts that "organizations learn only through individuals who learn. Individual learning does not guarantee organizational learning, but without it no organizational learning occurs" (*The Fifth Discipline*, p. 236). Chris Argyris and Donald Schon concur, noting that "individual learning is a necessary but insufficient condition for organizational learning" (*Organizational Learning*, p. 20). Individual learning, according to John Redding, is essential to the "continuing transformation of the organization, to expand the firm's core competencies, and to prepare everyone for an unknown future" (*Strategic Readiness*, p. 3).

Therefore each person's commitment and ability to learn is essential. Individual learning opportunities include self-managed learning, learning from coworkers, computer-assisted learning, daily work experiences, special assignments on projects, and personal insights.

There are a number of important factors that can contribute to increasing the power and impact of individual learning in the organization.

Individual and Collective Accountability for Learning. Everyone in a learning organization should be aware of and enthusiastically accept the responsibility to be a learner as well as to encourage and support the learning of others. Anyone and everyone can serve as a coach, facilitator, and resource for other employees/learners. They should also understand how these learning responsibilities benefit the organization. People should seek not only to teach but also to learn from their coworkers. The entire workplace should be filled with excited and accountable learners.

Locus and Focus of Individual Learning. Learning should be a constant in the work environment whether through on-the-job coaching, electronic performance support systems, action learning, or reflective planning. When classroom training is offered, it should be, whenever possible, provided in small just-in-time formats with immediate application to the job.

Accelerated Learning. Learning organizations seek to augment the ability of individuals to learn more information in less time as well as to increase learner retention through the many varied techniques of accelerated learning. Accelerated learning techniques engage all parts of the brain in the learning process in conjunction with both conscious and subconscious mental functions. This ensures that every means of learning and acquisition is utilized as simultaneously and fully as possible. Accelerated learning has also proved to be very effective in building innovation, imagination, and creativity into the learning process.

Some of the most powerful learning accelerators include:

- Mnemonics for greater recall and retention
- Music to engage the whole brain
- Metaphors to engage the whole learner for concept development and transfer of learning
- Peripherals to create a richer and more integrated learning environment

- Lighting, color, and room arrangements that can create receptive learning states
- Mindmapping or information graphs to aid learning, recall, concept formation, idea generation, and planning

Of course, different accelerators work better for different people. Learning organizations should therefore provide a variety of choices for learners. To enhance accelerated learning, a number of basic principles for enriching the learning environment can be considered:

- Provide a natural, comfortable, and colorful setting.
- Help people eliminate or reduce any fears, stresses, or learning barriers.
- Accommodate different learning styles, speeds, and needs.
- Present material pictorially as well as verbally.
- Treat learning as a collaborative effort of equals.

Bell Atlantic is one learning organization that recently established accelerated learning techniques for its customer service programs. The results were overwhelming. Training time was cut by more than half, trainers and learners were much more satisfied, job performance was higher, and costs were reduced by nearly 60 percent.

Personal Development Plan.   Individuals in learning organizations see learning as a way of life rather than a once-in-a-while type of event. They recognize that employers cannot guarantee them lifelong employment but that they can assist them in achieving lifelong *employability*. There should be a partnership between the organization and the employee to assist in the long-term career development of the employee. Organizations should be as up-front and open as possible in alerting the employee to future corporate directions and plans. Then the careful planning for self-development of the employee will make him or her a valued asset to the company. And if the company moves in a direction that no longer meets the skills or interests of the employee, the individual will possess competencies and know-how in demand at other organizations.

A number of learning organizations have developed excellent personal development packages for their employees. Caterair International has Passports for Success, Royal Bank of Canada guides employees with Planning Your Career, and PPG Industries utilizes a Professional Development Sourcebook.

Abundant Opportunities Available for Professional Development.
Individual learning in the learning organization is constantly encouraged, supported, accelerated, and rewarded through an organizational system that promotes continuous self-development and employability. Professional development opportunities exist for everyone in the organization, not just for managers. Resources include courses, workshops, seminars, self-learning materials, development groups, coaching, mentoring, and data banks. Employees are expected to learn not only skills related to their own jobs, but also the skills of others in their unit.

Individual Learning Linked to Organizational Learning in an Explicit and Structured Way. Learning is performance-based; that is, closely tied in with business needs. Learning is also an integral part of all organizational operations and processes. Individual learning, whether creative or adaptive, is transferred to the organization database for future transfer and application.

Group/Team Learning

Teams have become more and more important in organizations—whether they are running cross-functional projects, working on a manufacturing line, or reengineering business processes. In order to equip these teams with the knowledge and skills they need, learning organizations have taught them quality processes, problem-solving techniques, and team interaction skills.

As organizations must deal with increasingly more complex problems, they are discovering that they must become skilled in group/team learning. Work teams must be able to think and create and learn as an entity. They must learn how to better create and capture learning. Team learning can and should occur every time a group of people are brought together—whether for a single meeting, for a short-term project, or to address longer-term organizational problems.

It is important to recognize that team learning differs radically from team training. It is more than just acquiring group skills. The emphasis is on self-managed learning and a free flow of ideas and creativity. A successful team learning system ensures that teams share their experiences, both negative and positive, with other groups in the organization, and thereby promote vigorous intellectual corporate growth.

Teams should be able to generate knowledge through analysis of complex issues, innovative action, and collective problem solving. Teams need to learn better from their own experiences and past history. They should experiment with new approaches and quickly and efficiently transfer knowledge among themselves and throughout the organization.

As teams learn, they can become a microcosm of learning throughout the organization. Insights gained by the team are put into action. Skills developed can be transferred to other individuals and to other teams.The team's accomplishments can set the tone and establish a standard for learning for the larger organization.

Watkins and Marsick's team learning model (Figure 3-2) captures the relationship and learning among individuals, teams, and the organization. This model shows the learning organization as the union of individuals (the lower triangle) and organizations (the upper triangle). The key to this model is the overlap, which is where teams function and benefit the learning organization. The utilization of the combined resources and energies of the individuals, teams, and the organization is what creates the learning organization.

Learning organizations seek to create a full range of teams, including continuous improvement teams, cross-functional teams, quality management teams, and even organizational learning teams. These teams take time to reflect, to do action learning. They serve as vehicles

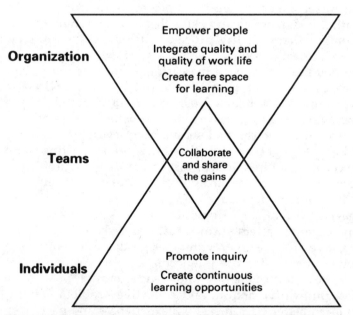

Figure 3-2. Team learning model. (*From Watkins, Karen, and Victoria Marsick*. Sculpting the Learning Organization. (*San Francisco, Jossey-Bass, 1993. Reprinted with permission.*)

for causing fundamental organizational change and renewal. Teams are encouraged not only to solve problems, but, according to Redding, to "generate fundamental new understanding of the business through a process of collective learning."

Team learning will occur more quickly and fully if teams are rewarded for the learning they contribute to the organization. Learning at the team level requires practice and reflection. High-level team learning enables high-level collective thinking and communication as well as the ability for working creatively and constructively as a single entity.

Organization Learning

Ray Stata, President of Analog Devices, distinguishes organization learning from individual and team learning in two basic respects. First, organizationwide learning occurs through the shared insights, knowledge, and mental models of members of the organization. Second, organization learning builds on past knowledge and experience—that is, on organizational memory which depends on institutional mechanisms (policies, strategies, and explicit models) used to retain knowledge.

Though individual/team learning and organization learning are interrelated, organization learning is seen as more than a sum of individual and/or group learning. Notwithstanding that individuals and groups are the agents through which the organization learning must take place, the process of learning is influenced by a much broader set of social, political, and structural variables. It involves the sharing of knowledge, beliefs, or assumptions among individuals and groups.

One way to show the difference between individual/group and organization learning is to consider a performing organization, such as an orchestra or basketball team. A symphony's performance or the winning of a basketball game cannot be attributed to individuals alone or even to the sum of individuals' knowledge and skills. It is the result of the know-how embedded in the whole group working in unison.

Types of Learning in Organizations

There are four types of learning or ways in which organizations learn: adaptive learning, anticipatory learning, deutero learning, and active learning. They are not exclusive of each other in as much as an individual or organization may employ more than one type of learning at the same time.

Adaptive

Adaptive learning occurs when an individual or organization learns from experience and reflection. The process in adaptive learning is as follows: (1) the organization takes an action intended to further an identified organizational goal; (2) the action results in some internal or external outcome; (3) the resultant change is analyzed for congruence with the goal; and (4) a new action or a modification of the previous action is initiated based on the outcome. Adaptive learning can be depicted as follows:

action → outcome → results data → reflection

Adaptive learning may be either single-loop or double-loop learning. *Single-loop learning* is focused on gaining information to stabilize and maintain existing systems. The emphasis is error detection and correction. Single-loop learning is concerned with obtaining direct solutions to the immediate problems or roadblocks (oftentimes, the symptoms) encountered by the individual or organization. Single-loop learning is by far the one and only loop learning used in most organizations today.

Double-loop learning is more in-depth and involves questioning the system itself and why the errors or successes occurred in the first place. Double-loop learning looks at deeper organizational norms and structures. It raises questions about their validity in terms of organization, action, and results.

Schein notes that most organizations and individuals are unwilling to engage in double-loop learning because it involves disclosure of errors and mistakes as well as the questioning of existing (often uncomfortable) assumptions, norms, structures, and processes.

Anticipatory Learning

Anticipatory learning arises when an organization learns from expecting the future. It is a vision-reflection-action approach to learning that seeks to avoid negative results and experiences by identifying the best future opportunities as well as discovering ways to achieve that future. This "planning as learning" approach is credited by Royal Dutch Shell as a highly valuable strategy for global learning and success that enabled them to handle a sharp drop in the price of oil. When that scenario occurred, they were the only oil company equipped with organizational skills and resources. Anticipatory learning can be delineated as follows:

vision → reflection → action approach

Deutero Learning

Deutero learning occurs when the organization learns from critically reflecting upon its taken-for-granted assumptions. Argyris and Schon, both Harvard professors and authors of numerous books on organizational behavior, call this "learning about learning." When a company engages in deutero learning, its members become cognizant about previous organizational contexts for learning. They discover what they did that eased or inhibited learning; they invent new strategies for learning; and they evaluate and generalize on what they have produced. The results become encoded and reflected in organizational learning practice.

In comparing the three types of learning described above, we can note that adaptive learning is more a coping form of learning. Anticipatory learning and deutero learning, on the other hand, are much more generative or creative types of organizational learning. When using these latter two types of learning, the organization is greatly empowered since staff is more proactive, reflective, and creative in their learning. Organizational learning may start as a reaction to events, but the proactive organization soon takes charge of its learning.

Action Learning

One of the most valuable tools for organizational learning is action learning. Action learning is the brainchild of Reginald Revans, one of the earliest architects of the concept of learning organizations, who began developing the elements of action learning more than 50 years ago. Over the years, a number of variations of the practice (e.g., action-reflection learning and goal-based scenarios) have emerged.

Action learning involves working on real problems, focusing on the learning acquired, and actually implementing solutions. It provides a well-tested method of accelerating learning that enables people to learn better and to handle difficult situations more effectively. Used as a systematic process, it increases learning in an organization so that the organization can more effectively respond to change.

For Revans, "There is no learning without action and no action without learning." The learning equation is: Learning = Programmed instruction (i.e., knowledge in current use) + Questioning (fresh insights into what is not yet known, or, $L = P + Q$. Action Learning builds upon the experience and knowledge of an individual or group and the skilled, fresh questioning that results in creative, new knowledge.

Groups of people normally use action learning to examine a difficult task or problem in the organization, act to change it, and bring back the results to the organization for review and learning. In action learning, people devote the quality time and energy necessary to learn how to learn and think critically. They build skills to meet the team or organizational needs that have emerged during the implementation or review of an organizational project.

There are two valuable benefits of action learning:

1. The development of skills and knowledge through the process of reflecting on actions taken when solving real problems

2. The organization change which occurs when participants address organizational problems from new perspectives

Action learning groups are different from task forces or quality circles in that action learning groups are charged with *learning* from the problems they are solving; assumptions are challenged, actions are confronted. In task forces the major goal is to address the problem, any learning that occurs is incidental. In addition, action learning groups often address unfamiliar problems rather than problems in which they have expertise, as might be more common in task forces. Addressing unfamiliar problems results in fresh perspectives being brought to bear on problems and provides individuals the opportunity to learn new approaches to address problems.

Principles and Skills of Action Learning. A number of proven principles of adult learning are demonstrated and practiced as people participate in action learning:

1. Our learning is increased when we reflect on what we did in the experience.

2. By relying solely on experts, we may become immobilized and not seek our own solutions.

3. We can learn critically when we are able to question the assumptions on which actions are based.

4. We learn when we receive accurate feedback from others and from the results of our problem-solving actions.

5. We are most challenged when we work on unfamiliar problems in unfamiliar settings—this is where the greatest learning may occur.

6. Nonhierarchical groups from across organizational departments and functions are oftentimes better able to gain new perspectives and therefore augment the learning.

7. Action learning is most effective when the learners are examining the organizational system as a whole.

There are also several key organizational learning skills that participants gain through the action learning process:

- New ways of thinking about the organization by addressing unfamiliar problems
- Self-understanding from the feedback of others in the groups
- Development of the skills of critical reflection and reframing which allow them to examine the taken-for-granted assumptions which have been preventing them from acting in new and more effective ways
- Teamwork skills by examining the way they function in the small group meetings and by having to work through the resolution of the problem

Action learning can be employed to address a wide variety of problems: complex problems that touch on different parts of the entire organization, problems which are not amenable to expert solutions, problems on which decisions have not already been made, and problems that are organizational rather than technical in nature. Examples of such problems could include the following:

- Reducing turnover in the workforce
- Improving information systems and reduction in paperwork
- Increasing sales by a predetermined amount
- Resolving a problem between R & D and production
- Increasing the use of computers in a company
- Reorganizing of a department
- Closing of a production or line
- Improving productivity in retailing or manufacturing companies

Action Learning Sets. The core entity in group action learning is the action learning set (group or team). The set is made up of 4 to 6 individuals who examine a complex problem that has no easily identifiable solution. The makeup of the group is diverse so as to maximize perspectives. Depending upon the type of problem, groups can be made up of individuals across functions, departments, or divisions. In some situations, groups are even composed of individuals from different organizations, for example, suppliers.

Though diversity is sought, it is important that group members be near the same level of perceived competence in order that members feel comfortable in challenging one another. Thus cross-level groups may be less effective. The dynamics of the group and the diversity of its participants are the keys to success of the action learning set.

General Electric and Action Learning

Several learning companies have made extensive use of action learning sets to learn and achieve organizational success. General Electric, for one, has declared action learning as a vital strategy in transforming GE into a global-thinking, fast-changing organization.

Action learning teams are built around GE problems that are real and relevant and that require decisions. Formats may vary, but typically, two teams of 5 to 7 people who come from diverse businesses and functions within GE work together on the project. GE has built into the action learning projects opportunities for feedback to the participants on strategies and on issues regarding their leadership and teamwork skills. The participants also have the opportunity to reflect on the total learning experience.

Besides team building, action learning has supplied GE participants with a context for dealing with multicultural and global issues. Global action learning teams usually focus on potential new GE markets. In a recent executive development course for global business leaders in Heidelberg, Germany, the action set spent the first week building team/leadership effectiveness and meeting with key European business leaders, opinion makers, and government officials from France, Germany, and Sweden.

During the second week, the focus shifted to projects from GE's plastic, lighting, and electrical distribution and control businesses. One action learning team looked at the lighting strategy for Europe, reflecting the sharp rise—from 2 to 18 percent in only 18 months—in GE's share of the western European consumer lighting market, mostly resulting from the acquisition of Tungsram in Hungary and Thorn Lighting in the United Kingdom. The teams were encouraged to be creative and think of serious ways in which GE could change the market and excite retailers and customers by finding new ways to add value. The participants traveled across Europe to conduct interviews, experience firsthand the effects of local culture, language, currency, legislation, and tax laws—and consumer preferences for national brands. Between interviews, the participants debriefed each other and prepared their final reports to present to GE leadership, including GE's CEO Jack Welch.

James Noel, manager of executive education at GE at the time of these action learning projects, has stated that action learning was pivotal in building GE into a learning organization. Action learning has made "participants active partners in the learning process. Because the team projects provide value to GE's businesses, it has an immediate return on investment. Action learning also provides a viable vehicle for dealing with issues of leadership and teamwork" (*Training and Development*, July 1992, p. 33).

Learning Skills/Disciplines

In his classic *The Fifth Discipline*, Peter Senge identified five learning disciplines or skills that would facilitate the transition of a company to a learning organization. To these five disciplines (systems thinking, personal mastery, team learning, mental models, and shared vision), I have added dialogue.

Systems Thinking

At a very early age in life, we are taught to break apart problems, to fragment the world. This appears initially to make complex tasks and subjects more manageable, but we pay a hidden, enormous price. We can no longer see the consequences of our actions; we lose our intrinsic sense of connection to a larger whole. When we then try to see the big picture, we try to reassemble the fragments in our minds, to list and organize all the pieces. The task is futile—similar to trying to reassemble the fragments of a broken mirror.

Systems thinking is a conceptual framework to help make full patterns clearer and to help us see how to change these patterns more effectively. It is a "discipline for seeing wholes," says Senge, "a framework for seeing interrelationships rather than linear cause-effect chains, for seeing underlying structures rather than events, for seeing patterns of change rather than snapshots" (*The Fifth Discipline*, p. 68).

High leverage changes are usually not obvious to most participants in the system. They are not close in time and space to obvious problem symptoms. Systems thinking, however, shows that small, well-focused actions can sometimes produce significant, enduring improvements, if they are in the right place, through leverage. Tackling a difficult problem is often a matter of seeing where the high leverage lies, and making a change which—with a minimum of effort—would lead to lasting, significant improvement.

Systems thinking, and particularly, system dynamics, can be a very powerful tool to facilitate organizational learning. Systems dynamics recognizes that organizations are like giant networks of interconnected nodes. Changes, planned or unplanned, in one part of the organization can affect other parts of the organization with surprising, often negative consequences.

Personal Mastery

Personal mastery refers to a special level of proficiency, similar to that of the master craftsman who is committed to lifelong learning so as to continually improve and perfect his or her skills. It is a discipline of continually clarifying and deepening one's personal vision, energies, and patience. Senge sees personal mastery as an essential cornerstone of the learning organization, since an organization's commitment to and capacity for learning can be no greater than that of each individual member.

Personal mastery entails a commitment to continuous learning at all levels of the organization. This includes the pervasive support of any kind of development experience for members of the organization. Mere presence of traditional training and development activities is not considered sufficient; these activities must be accompanied by a palpable sense that one is never finished learning and practicing, akin to the tradition of the Samurai, who never completes his quest for perfection.

Few organizations encourage the personal mastery of all their people. The result is a vast pool of untapped resources, people who have lost their commitment, their sense of mission, and the excitement with which they started their careers. Little of the energy and spirit that is required to rigorously develop the employee's or a company's personal mastery survives.

Team Learning

Team learning (the skill, not the level as described above) focuses on the process of aligning and developing the capacity of a team to create the learning and results that its members seek.

Most groups do not learn. The fundamental characteristics of relatively unaligned groups is frustration and wasted energy. Individuals may work extraordinarily hard, but their efforts do not translate into an efficient team effort.

By contrast, when a team becomes more aligned, a commonality of direction emerges, and individuals' energies harmonize. There is less wasted energy. In fact, as Senge notes, "a resonance or synergy develops, like the coherent light of a laser rather than the incoherent and scattered light of a light bulb" (*The Fifth Discipline*, p. 234).

Team learning involves the need to think insightfully about complex issues so that teams may learn how to best tap the potential of many minds. To become more intelligent than one mind, there is a need for innovative, coordinated action. Outstanding teams in organizations develop the operational trust where each team member remains conscious of the other team members and can be counted on to act in ways that complement the actions of other team members. This is how championship sports teams and great orchestras work and learn together.

There are three necessary ingredients for team learning to transpire:

1. The need to think insightfully about complex issues so that teams may learn how to tap the potential for many minds to become more intelligent than one mind
2. The need for innovative, coordinated action
3. The ability to encourage and stimulate learning in other teams

Mental Models

A mental model is our image or perspective of an event, situation, activity or concept. It is a deeply ingrained assumption that influences how we understand the world and how we take action. For example, each of us may have a different mental model of *school* or *father* or *government* based upon our previous experiences, perceptions, or upbringing.

Mental models of what can or cannot be done in different situations vary tremendously from person to person, and are often deeply entrenched and difficult to change. Senge stresses that the discipline of working with mental models starts with the individual and organization turning the mirror inward, of learning how to unearth internal pictures or images of the world and then to bring them to the surface and hold them rigorously to scrutiny. It includes, says Senge in *The Fifth Discipline*, the ability "to carry on learningful conversations that balance inquiry and advocacy, where people expose their own thinking effectively and make that thinking open to the influences of others." (p. 9)

Shared Vision

A shared vision provides members of an organization with the stars to steer by. It is hard to think of any organization that has achieved and sustained some measure of greatness without a deeply shared vision. Taco Bell has *number one in the stomach*, Federal Express has *absolutely*, *positively overnight*, and Polaroid has *instant photography*. Each of these organization are able to bind people together around a common identity and sense of destiny.

When there is a truly shared, genuine vision, people tend to excel and learn, not because they are forced to do so, but because they sincerely want to. It cannot be solely a personal vision of a charismatic leader, but rather a shared picture for everyone of the future. Such a shared vision fosters a heartfelt commitment by people throughout the organization to seek to improve, to learn, so that the vision can be achieved.

A shared vision is valuable for the learning organization since it provides a focus and energy for learning. While adaptive learning is possible without a shared vision, generative learning, according to Senge, occurs "only when people are striving to accomplish something that matters deeply to them."

Dialogue

Dialogue is intense, high-level, high-quality communications, listening, and sharing. It requires the free and creative exploration of subtle issues, a deep listening to one another, and the suspending of one's own views.

The discipline of dialogue involves learning how to recognize the patterns of interaction in teams that promote or undermine learning. For example, the patterns of defensiveness are often deeply ingrained in how a group of people or an organization operates. If unrecognized or avoided, they undermine learning. If recognized and surfaced creatively, they can actually accelerate learning. Dialogue is the critical medium for connecting, inventing, and coordinating learning and action in the workplace.

The discipline of dialogue is central to organizational learning since it promotes collecting thinking and communication. Dialogue (a) enables organizations to better tap the collective intelligence of groups, (b) equips us to see the world as a quantum whole rather than as fragmented parts, and (c) forces us to focus on uncovering and inquiring into how and why internal perceptions influence how we perceive reality. Schein depicts the difference between dialogue and the concepts of "discussion," "debate," and other communication processes as shown in Figure 3-3.

In successful dialoguing, people have the ability to:

- Recognize leaps of abstraction (when they are jumping from an observation to a generalization)

Suspension	Discussion
Internal listening, accepting differences, building mutual trust	Advocacy, competing, convincing
Dialogue	Dialectic
Confronting own and others' assumptions, revealing feelings, building common ground	Exploring oppositions
Metalogue	Debate
Thinking and feeling as a whole group, building new shared assumptions and culture	Resolving by logic and beating down differences

Figure 3-3. Ways of talking (conversation/deliberation).

- Expose what they are not saying while they are in conversation
- Balance inquiry and advocacy
- Face up to distinctions between espoused theories (what they say) and theories-in-use (the implied theory or image in what they do)

Learning Capacity of Organizations

John Redding, author of *Strategic Readiness: The Making of a Learning Organization*, has identified three dimensions to consider as one builds the learning capacity of the organization:

Speed of Learning, which refers to how fast the organization is able to rotate around the learning cycle (i.e., planning, implementing, and reflecting) and complete the iteration.

Depth of Learning, which refers to the degree to which organizations are able to learn at the end of each iteration of the cycle by questioning underlying assumptions and improving their capacity to learn in the future.

Breadth of Learning, which is concerned with how extensively organizations are able to transfer the new insights and knowledge derived from each iteration of the learning cycle to other issues and parts of the organization.

Training	Learning
Outside in, done by others, assumes relative stability	Inside out, seek to do for self, assumes continuous change
Focuses on knowledge, skills, ability, and job performance accomplishment	Focuses on values, attitudes, innovation, and outcome
Appropriate for developing basic competencies	Helps organizations and individuals learn how to learn and create own solutions
Emphasizes improvement	Emphasizes breakthrough (metanoia)
Not necessarily linked to organization's mission and strategies	Directly aligned with organization's vision and requirements for success
Structured learning experiences with short-term focus	Formal and informal, long-term future -oriented, learner-initiated

Figure 3-4. Training and learning contrasts.

Learning and Training

In learning organizations, we are now witnessing a paradigm shift in emphasis from training to learning. Training signifies a one-way trans-fer of established wisdom or skill from the expert instructor, while learning reverses this process in several important ways. Learning involves not only absorbing existing information, but also creating new solutions to problems that are not yet fully understood. Learning can take place in the absence of a teacher since it is an ability of the person, the group, and the organization. Some of the significant con-trasts between training and learning are shown in Figure 3-4.

Walter Kiechel, *Fortune* editor and commentator on learning organi-zations, sees learning and training as being the difference between putting the information out there for the employees to pick up (train-ing) and encouraging them to puzzle, wonder, and figure things out on their own (learning).

Organization Leader in Learning Dynamics—Arthur Andersen

In 1993 the Arthur Andersen Worldwide Organization became the world's largest firm in both accounting and in management consult-ing. Revenues exceeded $6 billion, double the amount collected in

1988. Nearly 70,000 employees work at Arthur Andersen's 324 offices in 72 countries.

Founded in 1913 by Arthur Andersen, an orphan of Norwegian parents, the company grew rapidly, first in the United States and soon in every part of the world. In 1989 Andersen reconfigured into two distinct units: Arthur Andersen & Co., which provides auditing, business advisory services, tax services, and specialty consulting services; and Andersen Consulting, which provides strategic services and technology consulting.

From its earliest days, Andersen has consistently strived to hire the best people the company could find and then to provide them with the best training available. A high standard of quality service to all customers has always been a trademark of the company. In addition, Andersen has long been an innovator among the major accounting firms. To further assure and expand the learning quality of its staff, Andersen opened its Center for Professional Education in St. Charles, Illinois, in the early 1970s.

Andersen's commitment to people, quality, and learning can be seen in examining the firm's vision statement (see Andersen's Vision statement, p. 51). Having a clearly defined vision, Andersen believes, is critical to organizational learning and achieving business success.

As the Company entered the 1990s, Andersen quickly recognized the changing environment and the need to learn even better and faster. Andersen's leaders realized that continuous learning and improvement is a strategy critical for organizational success. Nothing was seen as being more important to Andersen than to "exceed our client's expectations" and to sustain the company's long-term reputation for quality and innovation.

Becoming a learning organization and a leader in the subsystem of learning dynamics was therefore a natural evolutionary progression for Andersen. Let's review the many, exciting steps Andersen has climbed on its journey toward learning as an organization.

Paradigm Shifts from Business to Learning

The first major "learning organization" change made by Andersen was to request staff to make a paradigm shift in how they perceived their roles, environment, and everyday activities. Everyone was encouraged to transform their old businesslike mental model of supervisors, workers, activities, and office into the new learning-oriented mental model shown in Figure 3-5, which was printed on a 3 × 5 card and distributed to staff.

Old	New
Supervisors	Coaches
Everyone	Continuous learners
Engagement	Learning opportunities
Office	Continuous learning environment

Figure 3-5. Paradigm shifts at Andersen.

Shift from a Training to a Learning Focus

Until recently, Andersen's focus, like the training in most companies, had been on making instruction more efficient. The training focus was on the content and instructor, on the pace, and on getting the right answer. This transmittal training was based on the following assumptions:

- All learners have the same basic entry-level knowledge and skills
- People learn things in the same way
- Listening is the same as learning
- Changes can be produced more efficiently by focuses on observable behaviors than on ways of thinking

With this old model, there is no real concern for what is happening to the learner internally, whether he or she is either bored or overwhelmed with the pace of the instruction. The learner often does not fully understand the content being taught, and therefore cannot apply it.

A few years ago, Andersen decided that it needed a new approach to its professional education, that the training approach described above needed to be reengineered. Only with a radical change in training methodology and strategy could Andersen meet the five newly identified critical training and education requirements, namely: (1) develop broader and deeper skills, (2) build specialists who would be able to deliver seamless service to clients, (3) focus on business process change and integration, (4) balance common and unique skill development, and (5) adapt to complexity and continual change.

The new learning model at Andersen recognizes that learning the *process* of getting the right answer is the most important issue. The critical task is how to make the learning more efficient and effective. This new model of staff development at Andersen centers on the learner who, as a decision maker, chooses from among various available tools

ANDERSEN'S VISION STATEMENT

To be one global firm committed to quality by having the best people with knowledge capital, partnering with best clients to deliver value.

This vision encompasses seven components:

One Global Firm

We blend the strengths of our national cultures with the access to skills from around the world to serve clients anywhere. We provide clients with the same high level of service no matter where they are located.

Commitment to Quality

Our number one goal in service delivery is quality. Our people are empowered and expected to contribute toward this goal. Our success will be determined by the satisfaction of our clients.

Best People

Having the best people begins with attracting great people. Once we attract the best, we further train and develop them into an unparalleled team of outstanding professionals.

Knowledge Capital

We share the knowledge that resides in each of our people to assure our clients access to our best thinking. The focus of our business is our creative knowledge and our ability to distribute it globally.

Partnering

We want our clients to view us as a part of their team as we help them surmount their competitive challenges. As a partnership, we understand the value of teamwork.

Best Clients

We want to work with clients who want to get better, not just maintain the status quo.

Deliver Value

We deliver practical, leading-edge solutions with reliability and integrity. When we mutually agree that the client is better off for having procured our services, we know that we are delivering value.

and resources to learn what he or she needs for success. The emphasis is on the learning needed by the learner. The former role of instructor/presenter has been shifted to coach/mentor/facilitator.

According to Joel Montgomery, an education specialist at Andersen's Center for Professional Education, learners are now "much more active in the learning process, and are jointly responsible for their learning. Learners are asked to use what they have learned rather than repeating or identifying what they have been exposed to."

Andersen now designs its learning programs in a way that stimulates the learners to engage in activities that allow them to focus their learning on what they know they need. In the process, they are given the tool to reflect on what they are doing, to evaluate it according to some standard, and to give and receive feedback about what they are doing and learning. After they have gone through the process once, Montgomery notes, "We again stimulate them to reengage in learning, bringing with them what they learned the first time, again reflecting on, evaluating, and giving and receiving feedback on what they are doing and learning. This ensures a greater depth of learning."

This view of learning focuses on what happens to the learner internally, and it encourages increased sensitivity to the learner while instruction takes place. The instructional approaches are adjusted to meet the individual learner's needs. This represents a paradigm shift from a supply-push instructional approach to a demand-pull approach.

Self-Study, Point-of-Need Learning

To promote and enable continuous self-development, Andersen is focusing more and more on delivering self-study, point-of-need training that provides staff with opportunities to learn by doing and to develop individual skills. Since an individual's training needs typically derive from his or her current job assignments, accessible-upon-demand skill training has become increasingly important.

Andersen training features built-in flexibility for developing critical job skills at the individual level. Focus is on the increasing need and benefits of individualized self-paced instruction as determined by the learner. Instruction must increasingly be provided on a just-in-time basis, since most learning will need to occur just prior to the time such knowledge and skills must be applied.

By coupling technology with new learning strategies, Andersen has successfully developed interactive multimedia self-study training that is significantly more effective than traditional instructor-led training. Andersen has demonstrated to itself that it is possible to develop effective skills-building training within a self-study format.

According to Andersen, a key pathway to personal mastery is the development of metacognitive skills, where individual learners learn how to learn. The firm recognizes that the more metacognitive skills that the individual can gain, the stronger his or her chances of keeping current with change.

Action Learning

Andersen has placed a high emphasis on learning from experience (including reflection) at all levels of the organization, even as the vehicle to build executive skills at the partner level. Throughout the organization, there are efforts to move action learning from just the training environment to the work environment.

An example of ongoing action learning built into the Andersen process is the *coaching and continuous learning framework* for learning between the supervisor (coach) and employee (learner), which covers planning, application, and reflection (see Figure 3-6).

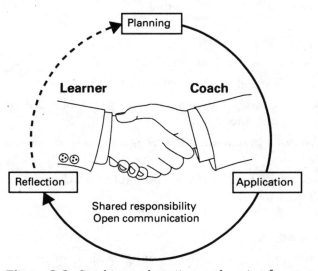

Figure 3-6. Coaching and continuous learning framework. (*Copyright © Arthur Andersen, Arthur Andersen & Co., S.C. Used with permission. All rights reserved.*)

Planning (between coach and learner, but as learner-driven as possible)

- Determine the gap between the learner's existing skills/knowledge and those demanded by the engagement (learning opportunity).
- Develop learning objectives and a plan to meet those objectives.
- Complete any pretask learning identified.

Application

Coach's Main Responsibilities

- Coach the learner based on the learning needs (job-specific, functional, adaptive).
- Provide the learner with needed opportunities.
- Make sure the learner has access to references and tools.
- Provide guidance and feedback when needed.

Learner's Main Responsibilities

- Apply the skills/knowledge acquired.
- Use the resources available.
- Reflect on current task being learned.
- Ask for assistance and feedback when needed.

Reflection

- Take the time to reflect on lessons learned.
- Determine how lessons learned can be applied in the future.
- Provide feedback on how well supervisors/supervisees did in regard to coaching and continuous learning.
- Discuss what can be done better, and also recognize and/or reward what was accomplished.
- Share what has been learned with others who might find the insight useful.

Collaborative Learning

Andersen has implemented collaborative learning, which consists of small group work where group members learn from one another by working together. This creates a rich learning environment in which the learner takes on various roles, including the role of the instructor. This approach promotes the sharing of ideas and knowledge and allows learners to review one another's work. It also allows them to coach, model, teach, and learn by using the abilities of team members and the team's synergy as part of the learning process.

Learning from Others—Global Best Practices

Andersen has placed a high priority on developing and utilizing a "global best practices" knowledge base. This knowledge base identifies and describes best practices, best companies, engagement experiences, studies and articles, performance measures, diagnostics, process definitions, and Arthur Andersen process experts.

More than 1000 CD-ROM discs of the knowledge base have been distributed worldwide. Global best practices workshops have been conducted for Andersen staff in offices around the globe. This knowledge base is a powerful learning tool for Andersen staff and also a valuable service that can be offered to clients.

Andersen also seeks to partner with "knowledge" firms so as to enhance its industry expertise. Recently Senn-Delaney, an international firm specializing in retail profit improvement, and Venture Associate, which specializes in the utilities industry, were contracted to work with the firm.

Participation in Conferences and Associations

Andersen has a deliberate strategy to gain and share knowledge through training, research, and participation in professional and trade associations. The company also produces publications for internal and external use with titles such as: *Retail Customer Satisfaction and Merchandizing, Physician Health Integration,* and *Vital Sign: Using Quality Time and Cost Performance Measures to Chart Your Company's Future.*

In order to maximize the in-house transfer of conference participation, Andersen strives to have at least three staff members attend seminars or conferences identified as valuable for the firm. Serving as presenters at conferences is promoted not only for the reputation acquired, but also to enhance the quality preparation, research, and learning skills of the participant.

Technology for Learning

Andersen recognizes that its continued global success is dependent on the technology skills that the company has developed and fostered.

The firm considers its client-service technology capability as one of its most powerful competitive weapons.

In 1994, the firm opened the Andersen Consulting Center for Strategic Research in California's Silicon Valley, intentionally near other technology innovators, thereby quickening the ability of Andersen to influence and apply the latest developments from these leading technology and research organizations. An initiative already under way is *Infocosm*, which is the creation of a working model of the information highway.

To facilitate the exchange of the firm's knowledge capital, Andersen developed a team to create and implement a knowledge capital delivery system. Expected to be one of the largest knowledge exchange applications ever developed, the system will store and disseminate Andersen Consulting's methodologies, industry best practices, and reference materials.

Excel through Learning Strategy

To achieve its corporate mission, Andersen developed its excel through learning strategy. Andersen decided that it must incorporate advanced technologies that enable diverse training development and delivery, powerful and effective education theories and best practices, and a performance support approach that ensures training timeliness and relevance.

Goal-Based Scenarios

Andersen has recently introduced goal-based scenario (GBS) training. The core of GBS is a simulated task that makes clear to participants what skills they need and why; what problems they are likely to encounter, and when; what is the most effective means of dealing with those problems, and why they are effective. Teaching and learning always takes place within the context of a clearly perceived need, as part of a larger task. GBS provides a motivational framework that serves not only to facilitate the acquisition of individual skills and facts, but also to enable students to understand how these skills and facts can solve client business problems.

Originated by Roger Schank, director of the Institute for Learning Sciences at Northwestern University, GBS is not simply a realistic simulation of some problem situation. Rather, as Andersen associate partner Alan Nowakowski states, GBS is "an artifice, carefully constructed to teach specific skills, lessons, knowledge, and abilities. And it must be executed in a manner that will in fact ensure that these things are learned by participants. For instance, this means that the unfolding of the scenario must be controlled so that learners see all of the important consequences of their actions, good and bad."

GBS contains the following components:

1. Learners are presented with an end goal that is motivating and challenging.

2. This goal is structured such that, in order to successfully meet it, learners are required to build a predetermined core set of skills and knowledge.

3. The environment is holistic. Skills and knowledge are taught as part of an integrated whole.

4. The learning environment is designed to take advantage of the different sets of experiences, cultural backgrounds, interests, and motivations of the learners.

5. Learners are able to explore and develop other than the predetermined set of skills.

6. Learners have the freedom to select their own strategies for meeting the end goal.

7. The stress level is appropriately managed by including a reflection, a genuine focus on the learning, and the availability of easy-to-use resources that support the learner's pursuit of the end goal.

JOB DESCRIPTION
ADVANCED LEARNING COACH
IN TAX EDUCATION FOR ANDERSEN CONSULTING

Background

Dramatic and fast-paced changes are occurring in the tax practice, in its customers, and in the field of learning. Tax education needs a focused way to provide leading-edge learning approaches to meet and anticipate the needs of the tax practice and its clients.

We are entering the age of high connectivity. We are no longer limited to the simple choices of self-study, instructor-led classrooms, or on-the-job learning options. Advances in technologies and learning theories have expanded our choices dramatically. We're seeing an almost endless variety of learning options to integrate into our training strategies. There are many opportunities to implement existing options and improve the learning process for our professionals. Improvement should lead directly or indirectly to better performance on the job.

Position Structure

The advanced learning coach position is structured in the following manner:

1. Provide information on strategic educational practices
2. Act as a sounding board and a conduit for new ideas, strategies, and support networks
3. Actively support tax education vision
4. Link with other areas of PED (Professional Education and Development) and the external training/learning world

Role of Advanced Learning Coach

The role of the advanced learning coach is to provide individuals with information about strategic educational practices. This information is expected to serve as input toward decisions that will have a positive impact on the learner and the learning processes. This will be accomplished as follows:

1. Targeting research and strategic thinking related to the advancement of our products and services
2. Focusing on specific opportunities in the design and development of new programs
3. Working within our area—educating and keeping us up to date relative to new strategies for learning
4. Increasing tax education's working knowledge of innovative strategies
5. Increasing the opportunities for knowledge transfer between individuals, project teams, and other key contacts to stimulate team thinking

Time Allocation

Person will spend 50 percent of time researching learning approaches and maintaining/developing networks of individuals both inside and outside the firm who can assist us in bringing diverse, creative, and current thought on learning to our projects. The remaining 50 percent of the coach's time will be spent participating on project teams and coaching individuals on new strategies for learning.

8. Learners use the resources on an as-need, just-in-time basis.

9. The environment often includes real-world tasks, learners working in teams, and human coaches who are experts in both content and process.

As can be discerned by examining the learning dynamics described above, Andersen has identified and implemented a number of powerful corporatewide actions that have made them a leader in the learning subsystem.

Top Ten Strategies to Build Learning Subsystem

1. Develop Action Learning Programs Throughout the Organization

The experiences of many learning organizations have shown that the most effective way of dramatically increasing systemwide learning is to encourage and enable everyone to become involved in action learning. Time and effort are used to reflect on actions planned and taken to identify learnings—whether they be successes or failures, whether they be of a technical or process nature. An action learning program begun in one part of an organization would later filter throughout the organization and thus become a catalyst for organizationwide change and learning. In general, it is ideal if the action learning programs can begin wherever significant learning is possible and needed.

Action learning programs should include both day-to-day reflections of individuals and groups as well as, and more importantly, action learning teams (sometimes called learning groups or learning sets).

The typical sequence of activities for an organization to establish action learning teams is as follows:

- An organizationwide workshop is planned to ensure that managers and workers understand how action learning works.

- Problems are identified for action learning. The problems chosen should be those that are meaningful to participants and their jobs as well as important to the organization as a whole. They should also be problems for which employees could offer several viable solutions, rather than problems which could be better solved by an expert.

- Action learning teams are formed with four to eight people from diverse backgrounds and functional expertise. This diversity enables the learning teams to examine the problems from fresh and different perspectives. A facilitator/process observer also may be part of the team, although this is not absolutely necessary. The facilitator should be someone the team members do not already know, so that he or she can act somewhat independently of the group's culture.

- Learning activities are developed around the discussion and resolution of each project. This may include feedback, reflective analysis, brainstorming, etc.

- The action learning teams may meet on a weekly or biweekly basis over a period of three to nine months. The groups meet for a full or part day depending upon the nature of the problems and the constraints of the organization.

- After the project is completed, the facilitator helps group members reflect on their work so that they can learn more about how they identified, assessed, and solved problems; what increased their learning; how they communicated; and what assumptions shaped their actions.

2. Increase Individuals' Ability to Learn How to Learn

Even though most of us attended schools for 10, 15, even 20 years, we never learned how to learn. We struggled with how to remember facts and relationships; we forgot even faster; we did not understand the learning processes. And yet, according to Andersen Consulting and many other leading learning organizations and researchers, a key pathway to personal mastery and more powerful and quicker learning is the development of metacognitive skills, where the individual learners are learning how to learn. Only by increasing the individual's metacognitive skills will the individual be able to stay current with the changing workplace environment.

A few years ago, the American Society for Training and Development (ASTD) developed a program that focused on the building of four key learning skills:

- How to ask questions of new information.
- How to break up complex ideas and large tasks into smaller parts.
- How to test yourself to see how much you are learning.
- How to direct your learning to meet specific goals.

Metacognitive skills enable people to think through, understand, and use new information quickly and confidently; find patterns in information; and focus on information that is most important.

3. Develop the Discipline of Dialogue in the Organization

The discipline of dialogue is central to organizational learning because it enhances and augments team learning. Dialogue forces new ways of viewing the organization's assumptions, and allows for a "cool communications field" to deal with the "hot" change and chaos of the environment.

In order to dialogue, members of the organization should be able to do the following:

- Suspend assumptions and certainties

- Observe the observer

- Slow down the inquiry

- Regard one another as colleagues

- Have a spirit of inquiry

Workers should also have opportunities to practice dialogue with a skilled facilitator who would use the following format:

1. Organize the physical space in a circle for a sense of equality for participants.
2. Introduce the concept of dialogue and ask participants to think about an experience of good communication in their past.
3. Ask group to share their experiences and explore what characteristics made the experience a good communication.
4. Ask group to reflect on these characteristics.
5. Allow the conversation to flow naturally, with everyone having the opportunity to explore and share.

A number of key questions relative to dialoguing in your organization will probably emerge:

- What factors prevent dialogue (e.g., defensiveness, smoothing over, winner takes all)?

- How to draw on diversity as a resource rather than a source of conflict?

- How to build shared visions and reflect on ways of looking at the world?

- How to improve observation, listening, and communicating skills?

- How to avoid distortion of information and blocking of communication channels through listening and feedback?

- How to balance advocacy with inquiry as a means to overcome impasses?

4. Create Career Development Plans for Employability

The pace of change requires that each employee take a proactive stance toward learning. Every person should have a clearly articulated career development plan that outlines a combination of formal and informal learning activities he or she will complete, with a timetable for completing them.

Many learning organizations (notably, Royal Bank of Canada, Saturn, Arthur Andersen, and PPG) work closely with staff to develop an individual development plan (IDP) which can serve a number of purposes:

- Allows for individualized ways for employees to develop themselves—courses, self-learning, mentoring, etc.
- Provides for a sequencing of learning so employees learn what they need to know just before they are likely to apply it
- Instills in each employee a commitment to self-management
- Holds each employee accountable for achieving his or her learning goals
- Helps develop an employability that can stay with employees throughout their lifetime

The human resources department should be available for assisting the employee in identifying learning resources—courses, mentors, conferences, agencies—that could be available. Supervisors should encourage ongoing learning, provide time and support for outside learning opportunities, and assist in long-range planning.

5. Establish Self-Development Cash Programs

Perhaps nothing demonstrates commitment to self-development and continuous learning more than giving a small, no-strings-attached cash budget to individuals. One company has gone so far as to have divided its whole training budget by the number of staff and given complete responsibility for spending for learning to individuals. For several years Rover has given employees $175 per annum tuition grants, called Rover Employee Assisted Learning (REAL), for lateral personal development in business areas not specifically related to current job skills. For example, an employee in production can learn French or computing or chess. Every year nearly 5000 Rover employees use these grants. Encouraging employees to develop to their fullest potential around topics of personal interest to them creates a person who enjoys learning and is better prepared to adapt to future personal and organizational changes.

6. Build Team-Learning Skills

Teams are to learning organizations as families are to the community. Teams form the connection between individual and organizational learning. Therefore, organizations must be committed to team learning, growth, and development; they should seek to build teams that are able to create and capture learning.

Team learning can occur every time people are brought together as a group for a single meeting, for a short-term project, or to address longer-term organizational problems. Team learning enables the organization to recognize and capitalize on latent resources within its work force. The emphasis is shifted to focus on self-managed learning and a free flow of ideas and creativity.

There are a variety of ways that teams can learn; namely, through generation of knowledge, analysis of complex issues, innovative action, and collective problem solving.

A few specific steps to enhance learning in teams include:

- Establish team responsibility for learning.
- Reward teams for the learning they contribute to the organization.
- Develop and practice team learning activities.
- Guide teams through the form, storm, norm, and perform stages.
- Build capability to achieve metalogue in which the team is able to think and feel as a group, build shared assumptions and culture, and work creatively as one organic whole.

7. Encourage and Practice Systems Thinking

An absolutely critical skill required for learning organizations is the skill of systems thinking, i.e., the capacity to see and work with the flow of life as a system rather than dissecting and trying to fix the problematic parts. Thinking about the big picture yet seeing underlying, unexpected influences is a rare and difficult skill to develop, but essential to do smart quantum learning.

Encouraging people throughout the organization to use the following elements of systems thinking will be most valuable:

- Focus on areas of high leverage.

- Avoid symptomatic solutions and focus on underlying causes.

- Distinguish detail complexity (many variables) from dynamic complexity (when cause and effect are distant in time and space, and when the consequences over time are subtle).

- See interrelationships, not things.

- See process, not snapshots.

- See that a person and the problem are part of a single system.

- Recognize the difference between systems and fragmentation thinking.

8. Use Scanning and Scenario Planning for Anticipatory Learning

A primary purpose of ongoing scanning of the environment is to be prepared for future changes that are most likely to affect the organization. Those organizations which are best at anticipating the future and using such planning as a learning opportunity are the ones that will be most ready and prepared to adapt. One excellent method for anticipatory learning is the development of scenarios about possible futures faced by an organization. By monitoring key trends, accessing strategic research, and analyzing the data, an organization can better determine what is important to learn.

Royal Dutch Shell employed this technique in advance of the oil crisis of the 1980s. When oil prices were still $28 a barrel, Shell created a scenario of what the world would be like if oil was $15 a barrel. Corporate planners constructed strategies, focused on learning requirements, and anticipated what changes would be necessary at the much lower price. When the actual price drop came, Shell was already knowledgeable about the world of $15-a-barrel oil. That anticipatory learning in the 1980s propelled Shell from the back to the front of the oil companies, where it has since stayed.

9. Encourage/Expand Diversity, Multicultural and Global Mindsets and Learnings

Learning organizations realize that different and various views and ways of doing things are a source of richness rather than a problem. The more we are open to new values, ideas, and perspectives in others, the greater the possibilities for individual and corporate learning.

Diversity initiatives work best when they are integrated into a larger system of business practices—total quality management, team building reengineering, and employee empowerment, which all have in common a commitment to continuous learning.

10. Change the Mental Model Relative to Learning

Most people still retain a negative picture of learning, one acquired in their school days—hard work, impossible tests, tough teacher, irrelevant education, control, memorization, drills, tests, long hours at their desks, etc. These images or mental models cause many people to resist adopting the lifelong commitment to learning required of those belonging to a learning organization. Jim Gannon, vice president of human resource at Royal Bank of Canada, states that the bank is reluctant to use the term *learning* because of the negative associations employees have with their school learning experiences.

Unless the mental model of learning changes, the efforts of senior management to build a learning organization will be doomed to failure, since their ideas will not be put into practice by workers. Because mental models are very powerful in affecting what we do, it is important to change the schoolroom mindset of learning to an exciting, collaborative, highly rewarding image. The mental model for learning organizations must be revisited with feelings of energy, excitement, business success, personal responsibility, fun, integration, sharing, and personal and organizational growth. Once this image of learning is established, individuals and organizations will want to jump quickly on the bandwagon.

Through training, management communications, and continual practice, organizations can help employees achieve a positive mental model of learning so that they are able to enthusiastically participate in the learning efforts of the organization.

4
Organization Transformation for Learning Excellence

The prime business of business is learning.
HARRISON OWEN

The organization is the structure and body in which and for which the individual, group, and organizationwide learning occurs. To go from a nonlearning to a learning organization requires a significant transformation, similar to the metamorphosis of the caterpillar. Along the way to becoming a butterfly, the caterpillar goes through some messy transitions. The raw protoplasm in the cocoon reaggregates (reforming, reengineering, restructuring, refocusing) and emerges as a beautiful and powerful butterfly that can fly in all directions—up and down, sideways, forward, and backward, able to flow with the wind or find safety from it.

The structure and strategies of a company must change almost as dramatically to become a learning organization. Faster and longer legs on a caterpillar will not be enough for the caterpillar to succeed in the competitive marketplace. To flourish as a learning organization, the company needs to reconfigure itself through an attentive focus on the four dimensions of the organization subsystem: vision, culture, strategy, and structure (Figure 4-1).

Figure 4-1. Organization subsystem.

Vision

A shared vision gives individuals and the organization the stars to steer by. It is hard to think of any organization that has achieved and sustained some measure of greatness without a deeply shared vision. Taco Bell's vision is to *become number one in the stomach*; Federal Express delivers packages *absolutely, positively overnight*; Polaroid provides *instant photography*. These organizations were able to bind people together around a common identity and sense of destiny.

The first and probably the most important step in becoming a learning organization is for people to build a solid foundation of shared vision about learning, accompanied by a recognition that unless the company becomes a learning organization, it cannot achieve its vision. There are many reasons why this shared vision of being a learning organization is so important:

1. A shared vision provides the focus and energy for learning. Vision causes people to do what they want to do. A vision represents their hopes and dreams, and provides meaning and value for them.

2. Without a pull toward some goal which people truly want to achieve, the forces on the status quo can be overwhelming. Vision establishes an overarching goal.

3. The loftiness of the target compels new ways of thinking and acting. It provides a rudder to keep learning process on course when stresses develop.

4. Powerful, generative learning occurs only when people are truly committed to accomplishing things that matter deeply to them. People with shared vision and values more readily question their established ways of thinking and their deeply held views.

5. Shared vision guides strategic thinking and planning for the organization; it can lead to multiple strategies and procedures for progressing on the path of being a learning organization. This occurs through the process of urging all stakeholders—managers, employees at all levels, customers, partners, shareholders—to become involved in developing the vision.

6. Creating shared values and meaning is important in determining what knowledge will be stored and transferred. This point will be examined in detail when we explore the knowledge subsystem in Chapter 6.

7. Shared vision fosters risk taking and experimentation. People become excited about trying new approaches to help the organization achieve its new vision.

Jim Gannon, vice president of human resource planning and development for Royal Bank of Canada, underscores the decisive importance of vision for learning as an organization when he says that "visions are what energize the organization"; they represent "the dreams that pull us forward."

Learning organizations are not machines, but living organisms. Much like human beings, they need a collective sense of identity and fundamental purpose. Visions should be exhilarating. They should create the spark and excitement to enable the organization to develop renowned, visionary products. Learning must be a part of that vision.

Culture

Organizations have distinctive ways of believing, thinking, and acting that are manifested by symbols, heroes, rituals, ideology, and values, collectively known as the *culture* of the organization. The nature of learning and the manner in which it occurs in an organization are determined in a large measure by the culture of that organization.

The culture of most organizations is one of nonlearning, if not antilearning. Taking risks, trying new approaches, sharing information, etc., are discouraged, while not causing any ripples gets rewarded. To become a learning organization, these cultural values need to be transformed.

Values complement the pulling force of a company's vision by being the pushing drivers that enable a company to reach the vision. A successful corporate learning culture has a system of values that is supportive of learning.

A Corporate Climate in Which Learning Is Highly Valued and Rewarded

Learning organizations provide a facilitative climate where learning is greatly encouraged and highly valued. Learners are the heroes. Learning gets recognized during performance appraisal time, at award ceremonies, and in the paycheck. Even pay-for-knowledge incentive schemes are established to reward employees for their learning.

3M provides an excellent example of a corporate climate that encourages and rewards learning. Workers are allowed up to 15 percent of their time to work on their own projects. 3M has also created the Pathfinder Award which recognizes those who develop new products or a new application of a product for a particular country or culture. In 1991 alone 67 different awards were conferred to different work teams—the value of those 67 creative ideas in terms of sales and creativity was $522 million!

Responsibility for Learning Is Shared by All

Employees have responsibility for their own learning and also for the learning of others. They must understand how their responsibilities relate to the goals of the organization as a whole. Employees are expected to teach, as well as to learn from, their coworkers. The entire workplace culture is geared to organizational learning.

Trust and Autonomy

People trust in and care for each other. One's inadequacies can be disclosed without fear of retribution. Learning organizations foster a culture of feedback and disclosure, where there are daily opportunities to learn from experience.

Managers see the facilitation of experimentation by the staff and the staff's learning from experience as one of their prime tasks. Managers also make time to seek feedback on how well they are facilitating learning.

Although there is a high degree of interdependence, people are encouraged to make decisions on their own in situations that require autonomous action.

Incentives for Innovation, Experimentation, and Risk Taking

Learning organizations take brave, bold steps to encourage as many people as possible to take risks, innovate, and get out of the habit of asking for permission and waiting for instructions. They realize that risks are necessary to achieve quantum leaps in product and service quality.

Responsible risk taking and an openness to new ways of doing things is promoted. There is no such thing as a complete failure—we can always learn from them. Mistakes are not only allowed, but valued, since they can be the source of new ideas and help people discover new ways of doing things.

In companies like Ford and Harley Davidson, the core values include intellectual curiosity, which means constantly challenging the status quo and looking for ways to improve learning and new ways to meet and exceed customer expectations.

Financial Commitment to Staff Training and Development

Learning companies make a strong commitment to providing financial and human resources to improve the learning quality of their staff. J. Y. Pillay, Chairman of Singapore Airlines went so far as to state that "our company's self-respect will be eroded, if we do not pay attention to the training needs of all our employees." The airline commits over 12 percent of total payroll costs to learning! Learning organizations such as Federal Express, Arthur Andersen, General Electric, and Motorola are not far behind.

Saturn spent significant amounts of money to conduct a comprehensive training program for workers even before production began. Workers received from 300 to 700 hours of training before entering the assembly line. The training continues afterwards in both technical and self-development areas. Saturn's 1995 goal is for workers to spend at least 5 percent of their work time, or 92 hours, in formal training.

Collaborative Creativity, Variety, and Diversity

August Jacacci, author of the article "The Social Architecture of a Learning Organization," sees a learning culture as one where there is "collaborative creativity in all contexts, relationships and experiences" and the measure of success is the combined wisdom and synergy of the organization as a whole. The whole culture learns in a self-aware, self-reflective, and creative way.

Operational variety is also encouraged so as to generate more and more ways to accomplish organizational goals. An organization that supports variation in strategy, policy, process, structure, and personnel will be much more adaptable when unforeseen challenges arise.

In learning organizations, different learning styles are recognized and appreciated. No single style is deemed as necessarily best, since an adaptive, innovative organization needs all styles, each of which can complement the deficiencies of the others.

Commitment to Continuous Improvement of Products and Services

Organizations committed to quality take continuous improvement seriously because one question is never far from the minds of everyone in the company: "How can this be done better?" Quality management requires continuous, comprehensive learning where everyone is constantly striving to do everything better. A learning culture seeks world-class standards in quality and service. There is pride and high self-esteem because of the high level of quality in service, products, and operations.

Responsiveness to Change and Chaos

In a learning culture, instead of a fear about constant change and chaos, there is an excitement and a determination to vigorously and creatively respond to such new challenges. Chaos provides the opportunity for "higher" levels of learning, for innovation, for breakthrough technology. As Harrison Owen notes, "Chaos creates the differences that make a difference, through which we can learn." (*Riding the Tiger*, p. 29)

Quality of Worklife

Learning organizations are committed to the development of the full range of human potential in an environment that invites participation and enjoyment. Work is exciting and challenging because one's mental as well as physical talents are being tapped. The social and physical surroundings encourage a respect for the total person. People care about each other.

CORPORATE LEARNING CULTURE AT CRAY RESEARCH

One company that has carefully spelled out its learning culture is Cray Research. Let's examine the company's corporate culture:

At Cray Research, we take what we do very seriously, but we don't take ourselves too seriously.

There is a sense of pride at Cray Research. Professionalism is important. People are treated like and act like professionals. But people are professional without being stuffy.

Cray Research people trust each other to do their jobs well and with the highest ethical standards. We take each other very seriously.

We have a strong sense of quality—quality in our products and services, of course, but also in our financial results and our working environment, and in the people we work with, in the tools we use to do our work, and the components we choose to make what we make.

Economy comes from high value, not from low cost. Aesthetics are part of quality.

We look first to our customers to define Cray Research quality— and we do our best every day to deliver it.

The effort to create quality extends to our shareholders, who invest in us to see a significant return, and to the communities in which we work and live.

The Cray Research approach is informal and nonbureaucratic, but thorough. People are accessible at all levels.

Communication is key. We stop by or call if we can. Keeping people informed is part of everyone's job. People also have fun working at Cray Research. There is laughing in the halls, as well as serious discussion. More than anything else, the organization is personable and approachable, but still dedicated to getting the job done.

With informality, however, there is a sense of confidence. Cray Research people feel that they are on the winning side. They feel successful, and they are. It is this sense of confidence that generates the attitude, "Go ahead and try it; we will make it work."

Cray Research people like taking responsibility for what they do and thinking for themselves. At the same time, we work together and are proud to share a single mission—to create the most powerful and highest-quality computational tools to solve the world's most challenging scientific and industrial problems.

Because the individual is key at Cray Research, there is a real diversity in the view of what we really are. In fact, Cray Research is many things to many people. Consistency comes in providing those diverse people with the opportunity to fulfill themselves and experience achievement individually and as part of the Cray Research team.

The creativity, then, that emerges from the company comes from the many ideas of individuals who are here and from the teams of Cray Research people who make these ideas into quality products for our customers. And that is the real strength of Cray Research.

Strategy

A number of powerful, leveraged strategies can be employed to quickly and successfully begin building the learning organization.

Intertwine and Align Organizationwide Learning with Business and Personal Success

Probably the most important strategy in inspiring and motivating the entire organization to quickly and emphatically move toward becoming a learning organization is to link increased learning with increased organizational success, to show that learning is the only source of sustainable strategic advantage for the company.

Businesses know that, in the long run, strategic and competitive advantages lie with organizations that develop core competencies that will enable them to create new products or services swiftly and thus adapt to rapidly changing opportunities. These core competencies, indeed, represent the collective learning of the organization.

Stephen Gill, author of *The Learning Alliance*, recommends that human resource development professionals link learning events and outcomes clearly and explicitly to business needs and strategic goals by undertaking the following actions:

- Map out the relationship between strategic goals and areas such as job behaviors, job skills, job-success indicators, and business objectives.

- Design prelearning activities, learning-event activities, and post-learning activities that are integrated into key business processes.

- Create an iterative process of delivery, feedback, and redesign for achieving timely learning and effective change as business goals shift.

Build Learning into All Operations and Activities

Learning organizations quickly and deliberately plan and structure learning into all organizational processes—design, manufacturing, marketing, accounting, etc. Firms that learn how to incorporate genuine learning processes in the fabric of practical work settings see dramatic results.

An example is a Ford Motor car-development learning laboratory that uses a computer stimulator and related tools to aid systems thinking as well as methods to enhance reflection and conversation. The laboratory helped a development team assemble a manufacturing prototype at full line speed—a first at Ford—which allowed advanced testing of assembly processes and was voted the highest quality ever by Ford's manufacturing organization. With the exception of minor adjustments, the vehicle was completed a record 10 months early!

The value chain of any organization should include a domain of integrated learning. This means thinking of the value chain as an integrated learning system. When thinking about each major step of the work process, beginning with strategic planning through to customer service, think of how learning experiments could be constantly engaged. Thus structures and process to achieve outcomes may be simultaneously viewed as operational tasks and learning exercises.

Organizations must fundamentally redesign work so that producing and learning are inextricably intertwined. Work should be considered practice and redesign, incorporating the continual movement between performance and practice characteristic of team learning in sports and the performing arts. Saturn has established such a setting at its worker development center, a learning laboratory adjacent to the assembly line that includes a complete mock-up of the assembly process.

If learning comes through planning and experience, it follows that the more one can plan guided experiences, the more one will learn. Until organizing for production at any stage of the value chain is seen as a learning experiment as well as a production activity, learning will come slowly. Managers need to learn to act like applied research scientists at the same time they deliver goods and services.

By systematically and intentionally building learning capacity through the integration of learning and producing, organizations are also building their performance capability.

Relate Staffing Policies to Becoming a Learning Organization

One of the most efficient ways to introduce and immerse an organization with learning and learners is through learning-rewarding personnel policies. Learning organizations recruit and hire people who continually learn, who enjoy expanding and exploring their potential. Staff who are dedicated learners and who enhance learning in people around them are promoted to supervisory positions. Nonlearners are encouraged to learn or seek employment elsewhere.

Recognize and Reward Learning

"That which gets rewarded gets done" is the maxim followed in learning organizations. Learners, especially learning teams, get promoted, receive bonuses, and are recognized and lauded. New ideas that lead to better services or products provide a "royalty" for their originators. People who collect and transfer knowledge from internal or external sources are commended. Performance appraisals look at learning acquired and distributed as much as at other actions of the individual. Teamwork is encouraged and the ability to build and motivate teams and team learning is highly rewarded.

Measure and Broadcast Impact and Benefits of Learning

Companies hoping to become learning organizations should develop a variety of ways of measuring learning. Focusing only on the typical measure of output (cost or price) ignores learning that affects other competitive values, like quality, delivery, or new-product introductions.

One of the most innovative and valuable tools to measure learning is the half-life curve developed by Analog Devices, a leading learning organization. A half-life curve measures the time it takes to achieve a 50 percent improvement in a specified performance measure. Companies that take less time to improve must logically be learning faster than their peers; and in the long run, their short learning cycles will translate into superior performance.

Generate a Large Number of Learning Opportunities

Generally, the more opportunities for learning that exist and/or are created the more learning occurs and the better it is. Learning organizations build in both the desire and opportunity to learn. Action-reflective learning is a regular part of day-to-day corporate activity.

Renowned specialists from inside and outside the organization are tapped either in person or through media such as video, audio, electronic mail, or teleconferencing. Learning forums are designed with explicit learning goals in mind. Strategic reviews and planning are seen as golden corporatewide learning opportunities. As people examine the changing competitive environment and the company's product portfolio, technology, and market position, learning is expected. Systems audits provide another opportunity for learning. Other learning opportunities include:

- Internal benchmarking reports, which identify and compare best-in-class activities within the organization

- Study missions, which are dispatched to leading organizations around the world to better understand their performance and distinctive skills

- Jamborees or symposiums, which bring together customers, suppliers, outside experts, or internal groups to share ideas and learn from one another

Set Aside Time for Learning

The creation of time for learning is one of the most important steps in building a learning organization. There must be time for reflection and analysis, to think about strategic plans, dissect customer needs, assess current work systems, and invent new products. Learning is difficult when employees are harried or rushed; learning can easily be lessened by the pressures of the moment. Only if top management explicitly frees up employees' time for this purpose does learning occur with any frequency. Of course, this time will be doubly productive if employees possess the personality and skills to use it wisely.

Create Physical Environment and Space for Learning

We are all aware of the impact of the physical environment on the quality and quantity of learning. We don't learn very well in noisy, crowded, dreary surroundings.

Physical architecture and space can be learning-oriented. For example, the removal of dividing walls; the construction of spacious and colorful central courtyards, atriums, and balconies; and the installation of many large windows are ways in which a company can provide sensitive and constructive artistry that serves learning.

A comfortable environment for learning establishes a physical setting that encourages sharing. It can also demonstrate the corporation's commitment to continuous experimentation as a means of institutionalized learning.

Maximize Learning on the Job

Most organizations now recognize that up to 90 percent of all learning occurs while a person is on the job. It is therefore highly leveraging for managers and workers not only to appreciate the learning that one is accruing, but also to create ongoing learning opportunities as well as build in a learning-reflecting mentality.

Ernst & Young has developed a successful continuous workplace learning model which attempts to capture as much on-the-job learning as possible. The two complementary aspects of the Model are shown in Figures 4-2 and 4-3.

The second component of the model guides staff in helping others to learn. One might suppose that this part of the model is for supervisors only. But that is not how it is used at Ernst & Young. The second component is for any employee helping any other employee, particularly a coworker, to learn.

The continuous workplace learning model is still very new at Ernst & Young and the firm is working at evaluating and implementing the model. Currently the company is using the model as the framework for a video on learning to learn. Ernst & Young is also trying to live the model; that is, staff goes through the process when it has new assignments or is challenged by a business problem. The company is also

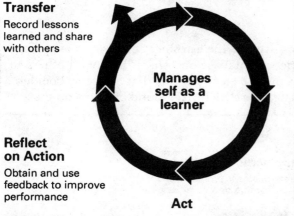

Workplace learning process

Use assignments, business problems and
experiences as learning opportunities

**Manages
self as a
learner**

Transfer

Record lessons
learned and share
with others

Plan

Identify what needs
to be learned to deal
with new and
unfamiliar situations

Ask questions
Identify and use tools
and resources to gain
knowledge

**Reflect
on Action**

Obtain and use
feedback to improve
performance

Act

**Reflect
on Plan**

Restructure problems
by incorporating
different perspectives

Figure 4-2. Ernst & Young continuous workplace learning model. (*Copyright © 1993 Ernst & Young LLP. Used with permission. All rights reserved.*)

MANAGE SELF AS LEARNER

- Use business experiences and problems as learning opportunities. These are the triggers for learning.

Plan

- Identify what needs to be learned to deal with new and unfamiliar situations.
- Ask appropriate questions and identify tools and resources to obtain knowledge related to business problems.

Reflect on Plan

- Restructure problems by incorporating different perspectives. This means you change your lens—frame and reframe the problem to look at it from a variety of ways.

Act

Reflect on Action

- Obtain and use feedback as tasks are executed and completed to improve performance. Reflect on how it went, assess how you did vis-à-vis your plan, and seek input from others so you can extract the lessons learned from the experience. Identify the learnings you didn't anticipate.

Transfer

■ Transfer the learnings—record the learnings so they become part of your business experience database and share them with others so they can build on them. Use electronic file diary, "events booklet," or put input into a data base structured around business processes.

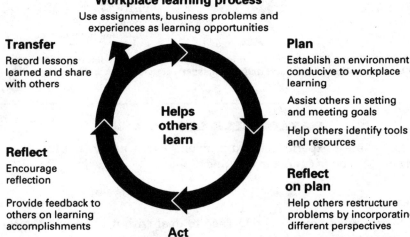

Workplace learning process
Use assignments, business problems and experiences as learning opportunities

Transfer
Record lessons learned and share with others

Helps others learn

Plan
Establish an environment conducive to workplace learning

Assist others in setting and meeting goals

Help others identify tools and resources

Reflect
Encourage reflection

Provide feedback to others on learning accomplishments

Act

Reflect on plan
Help others restructure problems by incorporating different perspectives

Figure 4-3. Ernst & Young continuous workplace learning model. (*Copyright © 1993 Ernst & Young LLP. Used with permission. All rights reserved.*)

looking into ways to incorporate the process in the way it designs learning activities.

The following directions for the use of the model are distributed to Ernst & Young employees:

The reasons for developing and improving our learning skills are compelling—the world is smaller and yet more complex, there is too much to be learned, information is easily accessed, and the business environments are constantly changing. Since the majority of our learning takes place on the job, we need to get consistently better at this kind of learning.

HELP OTHERS LEARN

- Use assignments and business experience as learning opportunities.

Plan

- Establish an environment conducive to workplace learning.
- Assist others in setting and meeting learning goals. This can occur as assignments are made or during a performance review when developmental needs are identified and goals are set.
- Help others identify tools and resources.

Act

Reflect on Action

- Encourage reflection. Help others reflect by asking questions to probe thinking about the action.
- Provide feedback to others on their learning accomplishments so they improve on their performance and capitalize on their successes. Timely feedback enhances the learning and lets people use the feedback on the next assignment or to solve a business problem.

Transfer

- Transfer the learnings. Record them so they become part of your business experience databank and share them with others so they can build on them.

The continuous workplace learning model provides a process for turning work assignments and business problems/opportunities into learning experiences. And what could be a better metaphor for this than the kaleidoscope—a lens for viewing a series of patterns through the reflection of an image produced by mirrors. Through planning, reflection, and feedback, we can develop a series of different "pictures" of how to deal with new, unexpected, and complex challenges facing us.

The continuous learning skills can help us respond to our clients' needs with better, quicker solutions if we consciously and intentionally learn from past experiences and new opportunities. By asking questions, looking at problems with a different lens, developing plans of action and reflecting on them, acting and then seeking feedback and reflecting again, and documenting what we learned, we can develop a systematic way of using the workplace as a laboratory for learning.

You can enter the model at any place to start the process. To simplify how it works, let's assume you have a new work assignment or a unique client business problem. Here's how the learning skills fit around the model to help you turn that opportunity into a learning experience.

Assist others in setting and meeting learning goals. This can occur as assignments are made or during a performance review when developmental needs are identified and goals are set.

Provide feedback to others on their learning accomplishments so they improve on their performance and capitalize on their successes. Timely feedback enhances the learning and lets people use the feedback on the next assignment.

Structure

Structure operates as a powerful directive force on a company's life and people. It determines the amount of internal control, the work organization, performance monitoring, lines of communications, and the decision-making process that will exist in the organization.

Although form should follow function, the opposite is very often the case; as a result, the form or structure of many organizations prevents them from ever beginning the journey toward corporatewide learning. Rigid boundaries, bulky size, disjointedness of projects and tasks, and bureaucratic restrictions all help to kill rather than nourish learning.

The structural characteristics of learning organizations, on the other hand, exude flexibility, openness, freedom, and opportunity. Boundaries are highly permeable, which maximizes the flow of information and opens the organization to its experiences. The firm's structure is based on the need to learn; the driving organizing principle is to put the necessary freedom, support, and resources in the hands of the people who need them. As tasks, needs, and people change, the structure changes so that customers and employees alike can optimally respond and grow. Ultimately, what best allows and supports learning and accessing knowledge are the guidelines for establishing corporate structure.

Streamlined, Flat Hierarchy

Rigid, tall hierarchies with unbreachable, impregnable department silos are a bane to learning as they prevent the necessary free, fast, and unimpeded flow of knowledge essential to being competitive. Power and authority are not able to flow to the point of greatest impact, further hurting the an organization's interest and ability to learn. To maximize the flow of knowledge and learning, a flat, streamlined structure with team collaboration and few modes of control works best.

Seamless, Boundaryless, and Holistic

A learning organization should feature fluid, boundaryless structures that have no respect for divisional barriers. Boundaries inhibit the flow of knowledge; they keep individuals and groups isolated and tend to reenforce preconceptions, distrust, and bias.

When people build a culture that is focused on maximizing the learning capability of the organization, they are able to build learning that crosses all boundaries—time, vertical, horizontal, external, and geographic. They possess a holistic, systematic view of organizational life with all of its systems, processes, and relationships. There is an integration, an intimacy, a closeness between management, employees, customers, competitors, and community. All these factors make it possible for learning organizations to better understand and appreciate the changing needs and successes of people in and out of the organization.

Project Form of Organizing and Implementing

More and more of the work of the future will be done by project teams, since project teams are better able to respond to and serve the needs and interests of customers. The life of a project team may be indeterminate or just a few hours. Dynamic, short-lived project configurations will be commonplace. It will not be unusual for employees to work with four to five project teams in a year and yet never work with the same group of colleagues. The smaller size, quickness, and accountability of project teams all encourage more efficient and more applicable learning.

Networking

Effective learning organizations realize the critical need to collaborate, share, and synergize with resources both inside and outside the company. The network structure, which may include global alliances, informal ties among teams that work across functions, and new ways for employees to share information, uses a variety of connecting tools such as management information systems and videoconferences. They provide a company with a form and style that is fluid, flexible, and adaptable.

A traditional corporate structure, no matter how decluttered or delayered, cannot muster the speed, flexibility and focus needed in today's highly competitive marketplace. Networks are faster, smarter, and more flexible than reorganizations or downsizings. A network, in effect, creates the small company inside the large company that is critical for organizational learning and global success. Networks differ from teams or task forces in that they:

- Are not temporary
- Do not only solve problems that have been defined for them, but take their own initiatives
- Can make substantive operating decisions on their own

Small Units with Entrepreneurial Thinking

Learning organizations, no matter their size, are structured like and operate with a dynamism and entrepreneurial spirit similar to that of new, small companies. Why? Because when the size of a working unit becomes too large, knowledge and empowerment get lost. Communications and commitment are lessened.

Asea Brown Boveri (ABB) is an excellent example of a large learning organization that has stayed small. With over $30 billion in sales per year and over 200,000 employees worldwide, ABB is streamlined into 5000 autonomous profit centers, each containing no more than 50 people!

Bureaucracies Are Rooted Out

General Electric is an example of a successful learning organization. In its Annual Report, written by John Welch, CEO, GE states its beliefs that "a passion for excellence requires hatred of bureaucracy and all that goes with it." Royal Bank of Canada believes that an organization should centralize paper but decentralize people. Staff should "roto-rooter out" silly forms and policies that gridlock and strangle learning. Fewer boundaries and fewer bureaucracies allow the lifeblood of knowledge to flow quickly and freely throughout the organization.

Hewlett-Packard, an innovative company which, in recent years, had become a lumbering dinosaur, decided to undo its growing bureaucracy which had become so encumbered that three dozen com-

Bureaucracy	Learning Organization
Short-term goals	Corporate and individual vision
Rigid culture	Flexible culture
Product orientation	Learning orientation
Regional emphasis	Global emphasis
Management direction	Employee empowerment
Procedure bias	Risk bias
Analysis only	Creativity, analysis, intuition
Competition	Collaboration and cooperation

Figure 4-4. Changing the organizational paradigm.

mittees oversaw every decision, delaying new products and crushing learning, speed, and innovation. Employees were urged to rethink every process from product development to distribution. The new lean, sleek learning organizational structure is now called a *gazelle* by industry leaders.

As a result of the dramatic changes undertaken in developing a new learning vision, culture, strategy, and structure, companies are transformed from a rigid, management-focused bureaucracy with a short-term orientation to a dynamic learning organization. Figure 4-4 provides a comparison of these two different paradigms:

Let us now examine and analyze Caterair International, a company that has demonstrated leadership in the organization subsystem of the learning model.

Leader in Organizational Transformation—Caterair International

Caterair International serves more airlines worldwide than any other airline caterer, with over 22,000 employees operating in 23 countries. Headquartered in Bethesda, Maryland, the company was formed in 1989 as a reincarnation of Marriott Corporation's airline catering division. Caterair controls about 40 percent of the domestic aviation catering market. It has a major global presence with 44 percent of sales coming from international business. Caterair has kitchens in Australia, South Korea, Japan, and Taiwan. It also has joint ventures overseas—in

Moscow with Aeroflot and in São Paulo with Varig. In 1994, Caterair catered approximately 200 million meals worldwide on approximately 2 million flights.

Caterair International clearly understands that in order to be the airline caterer of choice:

- Employees must experience a quality of life resulting from an environment of growth, fair treatment, and opportunity.

- Customers must receive value and consistent, superior service for the specified products.

- Airline passengers must perceive onboard food as a necessary and valuable feature.

- Shareholders must receive at least the required return on investment.

- The community must share and benefit from our success and perceive us as a good corporate citizen.

Becoming a learning organization was seen as the best pathway for Caterair International to meet the challenging expectations of these various stakeholders. Developing a learning vision, culture, strategy, and structure became the goal of Caterair people.

Vision and Values of Caterair as a Learning Organization

Caterair decided that a clear corporate vision built on corporatewide learning should become the cornerstone of its globally expanding organization. This vision of learning and organizational transformation would have to be an integral part of the company's documents, discussions, and daily life.

Caterair's vision and values provide a clear picture of the "stars to steer by" for the company. They also furnish the tools that Caterair would employ to fulfill its goal of being the learning leader in the airline catering industry.

According to David Workman, senior vice president of human resources, the company knew that the Caterair vision would be achieved only if there were agreement and strong support for the values underlying and supporting that vision. The values had to be developed organizationwide and everyone in the organization would participate in Caterair's new "mission, vision, values" training, discussions, and meetings. Top managers were trained to facilitate these efforts.

CATERAIR'S VALUES STATEMENT

Customer Driven

- Being the best in the eyes of customers is our #1 job.
- Treat each customer as if he or she is our only customer.
- There is no small customer or small customer base.
- All airline employees are our customers.
- Exceeding customer expectations in all we do.
- Solve customer problems...fast!
- Prevent problems from recurring.
- Make and meet every customer commitment.
- Do the customer's work as if you were doing it for yourself.
- Recognize improvements that lead to customer satisfaction.

Continuous Improvement

- Communicate the need—the intense competition in the airline business is making our customers demand more from us for the same money.
- Continually improve all that we do and how we do it—not only in big steps, but mostly in lots of little steps.
- Relentlessly pursue perfection—strive for zero defects.
- Don't think that you're the best because it's the enemy of getting better.
- Find ways to prevent problems before they happen.
- Replace "We don't do it that way" with "Let's try."
- Continuous improvement requires *continuous learning*.

Global Mindset

- Communicate the fact that the airline business has become a world-as-a-single-market business.
- Every unit is a member of the Caterair global team.
- Remember that one unit's performance affects the success of all other units on the global team.

- Pursuing the world market offers the opportunity to grow and further secure our livelihoods.
- Maintain a Caterair world standard of quality.
- Pursue business opportunities with every airline.
- Look forward to and accept career opportunities throughout Caterair's world.

Teamwork

- Teamwork is an attitude, not a collection of players.
- Communicate team goals.
- There are no wins without the team winning.
- Solve problems as a team.
- Recognize team accomplishments, not just individual accomplishments.
- Argue among ourselves but act with one voice.
- Think of the next person down the line as your customer.
- Think of yourself as the customer of the next person up the line.
- Pitch in and help others, even if it's outside your usual work.

A Learning Culture

Leadership at Caterair was determined to create empowered employees and build high-performance teams. Caterair management and staff developed a five-year strategic plan for the company formulated to serve both as a map for the future and as a blueprint of what must be done to remain the leading airline caterer in the world.

The company conducted a series of executive events to forge consensus and build learning teams. Management initiated a process to formalize the development of the strategic business plan; measured their corporate culture worldwide; redefined the corporate mission, vision, and values; and introduced a systematic decision-making process companywide designed to facilitate planning, problem solving, communications, and resources allocation.

Caterair's commitment to learning promises that "Every improvement by employees will earn recognition; breakthroughs will cause celebration." All managers are expected to provide guidance, encouragement, and assistance to their staffs to foster new learning.

Empowerment

The empowering motto of Caterair is "Caterair people can." Caterair realizes that this can occur only if and because the organization will:

- Tolerate no blockage of essential information
- Drive out fear and mistrust from every corner of the organization
- Always strive for world-class standards in quality and service

Caterair is very proud of its code of fair treatment, which pledges to ensure the same opportunities for individual growth and sharing of gains for all employees. Efforts were undertaken to drive mistrust from every corner of the organization and keep it out.

Management set the following rules for the treatment of employees:

- Respect our people's knowledge.
- Solicit problem-solving ideas from our people.
- Encourage unsolicited problem-solving ideas.
- Listen to ideas different from your own.
- Respond in a timely way to 100 percent of people's suggestions.
- Put decision-making power in the hands of the person who knows the most about the task.
- Give people the authority to act when they must.
- Back up the person to whom you gave the power.
- Find out why a mistake happens, learn from it, and prevent it from recurring.
- Forgive honest mistakes.

Role of Managers

Caterair managers see the development and learning of the people around them as their major responsibility. The guidelines for this role include:

- Treat all people with respect, honor, dignity and fairness—take care of the people.
- Recognize a job well done.
- Create an environment of continuous learning.
- Facilitate self-directed work teams.
- Help people feel free to ask questions.

- Supply people with the tools they need to do their work.
- Make and meet commitments to all our people.
- Increase our people's knowledge and skills.
- Encourage advancement and promotion.
- Increase confidence, self-esteem, pride, and professionalism.
- Seek out highly motivated people to join our team.

Passport for Success

Every manager at Caterair is given a "Passport for Success" booklet which allows them to receive a "stamp" as the various competencies are learned and demonstrated, just as if they were meeting requirements that enabled them to enter new countries. In the introduction of the Passport is the following advice to the Caterair manager:

"Learning is a continuous journey, not a destination. The learning experience, like a journey, takes place over time. As we move through life, we are exposed to new ideas, new challenges and new opportunities to learn. These learning opportunities help to broaden our experience and add to our value as managers. Learning is what keeps our work interesting and challenging. When we stop learning, we stop growing.

Caterair is a learning organization....the company has committed to a multi-faceted approach to helping its managers learn and grow. The intent is to foster a learning environment which will prepare our leaders to meet the challenges and react to the changes in our global business....Throughout the learning process, the focus will remain on how you can learn and grow."

A Learning Environment

Management at Caterair is trying to create an entirely new organization and learning environment so people can constantly learn, be innovative, and meet customer demands.

The human resources staff has worked hard to "change the essence of how we do learning at Caterair." Particular attention has been directed to the processes of how adults learn and how to disseminate skill sets.

The Caterair approach is to provide learning opportunities that are targeted to each level of the organization. With a goal of merging specific job-related skills and leadership development training, Caterair has established two separate but complementary training programs.

The Caterair Quality and Leadership Institute. The purpose of this program is to communicate, educate, train, and problem solve business issues, establishing a learning environment to sustain and support new culture and quality process. It concentrates on providing skills with which managers can improve individual work processes in their units or functional needs.

The Quality Institute offers 11 courses for employees ranging from new hires to future general managers. Altogether they provide a spectrum of learning opportunities tailored to the food service industry, ranging from statistical process control and Pareto analysis, group facilitation techniques, contamination and foodborne illness, and meal load factor determination to productivity measurement. The courses offered are:

- Quality Tools
- Group Facilitation Techniques
- Total Quality Management—Orientation
- Sanitation Certification
- Transportation Scheduling
- Productivity Measurement
- Quality Measurement Systems
- Customer Service Techniques
- Purchasing Management
- Production Systems
- Operations Finance and Administration

The Caterair Leadership and Development Institute. The focus here is more on providing managers with the leadership skills they need to change their working environment and to implement Caterair's values on a day-to-day basis. The purpose of this program is to expose management to techniques that will help them develop their subordinates into high performance teams and ready them for more senior positions.

Caterair management views the institutes as the primary driver of culture change throughout the organization, from the executive's desk to the airline kitchens. In an effort to streamline training and organization efficiency, Caterair combined production and food, service and transportation, and multiple and single kitchens.

Corporatewide Strategy to Build a Learning Organization

David Workman, senior vice president of human resources, recounts how Caterair realized that global success depended on the "need to change the essence of how we are learning. We needed a clear mission, vision and values that would buttress and serve as the foundation of employee development, and provide the energy and enthusiasm needed for organizational learning." He adds, "We are trying to create an entirely new organization and learning environment. Our people need to be able to constantly change so they can be innovative and meet customer needs. To gain a sustainable advantage, we produce top leadership and top quality."

People at Caterair talk about an operational triangle. The triangle is formed by Caterair and its customers and suppliers. The goal is that Caterair people will routinely exceed their customers' expectations for quality, consistency, and dependability. So that "our customers will offer us as an example to others." The standard is that "We will act as though each customer is our only customer."

Being customer-driven is a great incentive for learning. Caterair staff recognize that they are in a customer-driven business, and that "We do not so much have a product to sell as customers to be satisfied. In our quest for quality, two factors are paramount: we will strive continuously to improve, and we must be the best in the eyes of every person who works for our customer."

Caterair has created customer service teams that are located throughout the world. The teams are made up of specialists in quality assurance, marketing, pricing, billing, specification writing, and culinary and other catering-related areas. The goal of these teams is to maximize productivity and customer satisfaction. Much work has gone into transforming Caterair kitchens into customer-focused service centers with a high emphasis on staff training.

The customer focus combined with quality learning programs have produced exemplary service and customer satisfaction. Since Caterair began the program in the early 1990s, the company has compiled an average performance record of only one delay for every 4424 flights catered.

Communicating the Vision of a Learning Organization

Caterair uses its *Horizons* newsletter, which is published quarterly in six languages to promote the learning organization concepts. The company also publishes 12 regional newsletters, which focus on local events and celebrations. Managers also benefit from a videotape series produced for them in the second month of each quarter. The videos, which are made available in French, German, Portuguese, Russian, and Spanish, cover finance, marketing, and industry news.

Technology for Learning

Caterair recognizes that it is in a low-technology, service-intensive business. At the same time, management believes that the judicious application of appropriate technology can raise the level of service, produce higher quality, and promote lower cost throughout the company's worldwide network. Accordingly, Caterair has embarked on a program of technological improvement unique in its industry.

Trainees benefit from technology-based instruction. The 27-person human resource staff produces training programs using laser disc and satellite delivery, as well as conventional methods.

The company has also invested $14 million for new technology and improvements to the existing fleet and facilities. In the Caterair kitchens a series of new automated robotic systems is being phased in.

Reengineering for Increasing Corporatewide Learning and Profits

Reengineering and streamlining structure so as to increase learning and profits has become a top priority at Caterair International. A few years ago a task force was formed to review existing facilities and make recommendations designed to maximize resources, increase productivity, and sustain profitability. Radical redesigns were recommended and executed. As a part of the process, employees of Caterair go through extensive orientation and introduction into the importance of ongoing learning and continuous improvement.

After the reengineering mechanics were completed, support tools were instituted to maintain ongoing improvement. After careful recruitment and selection, new employees are oriented to a continuing learning process of assessment, development, evidence of accomplishment, and progress.

In addition to these efforts, Caterair also has put a reward system into effect that supports learning and continuous improvement as critical aspects of sustaining the dedication to quality assurance.

There is also a reengineering task force focused on what Caterair's kitchens should look like. They believe that in leadership and quality they have a sustainable advantage that cannot be duplicated by any other organization. Caterair is reengineering its units to reduce costs and cycle time while increasing productivity and profitability.

Caterair restructured in order to learn and to respond more quickly to the changing needs of the airline industry. "We're pushing decision making closer to the action. The organization is less centralized. It's going to unleash Caterair's talent and make for a more productive company and a much happier customer," says Dan Altobello, CEO of Caterair.

New Opportunities for Caterair International

Looking ahead, it appears that the worldwide air travel market will continue to grow through the 1990s, nearly doubling in size by the year 2000. Caterair expects consolidation within the airline industry to continue for several more years. CEO Daniel J. Altobello says, "Far from being a disadvantage, we view the twin phenomena of growth and consolidation as strengthening the industry and providing additional business opportunities for Caterair. The traditional partnership between suppliers and customers will grow stronger with growth and consolidation."

To be the "airline caterer of choice in the world" involved a commitment to provide employees with all the necessary tools and resources to deliver quality, consistency, and dependability. Caterair's successful steps in building a learning organization, as well as its reputation for quality and strong bonds with many of the world's airlines, will work to the company's advantage in the years ahead. Caterair International has quickly become a high-flying global learning organization.

Top Ten Strategies for Organization Transformation to Learning

1. Hold a Future Search Conference to Develop Vision of Learning Organization

A critical first step for becoming a learning organization is for leadership and as many of the various stakeholders as possible—employees, customers, suppliers, and partners to be involved in re-creating the company as a learning organization. Changing an organizational vision may feel like changing the tire of a moving car, but it is crucial that the old tire get removed and a new tire (vision) be installed.

The more people that are involved in shaping the vision, the clearer the vision will be and the more quickly it will become a reality. Future search conferences can, as Marvin Weisbord, author of *Discovering Common Ground*, notes, "bring people together to achieve breakthrough innovation, empowerment, shared vision, and collaborative action."

There are a number of principles and procedures that leaders should consider as they plan and conduct a search conference for building the learning organization:

- Participants explore, together, the *whole* system—its history, ideas, constraints, opportunities, global trends, sources, etc.

- Energy is put into the *common ground* that all can stand on without being forced or compromised, so as to validate polarities rather than reconcile them.

- Learning must be reinforced prior to and after the visioning search.

- The implementation and sustenance of learning depends on understanding and capitalizing on the resources of the entire environment and all systems.

- A key intervention is to create structures that facilitate relationships.

- Acting locally is a sound strategy for changing large systems, since everything is connected.

Core values necessary for the future search conference to successfully begin building the learning organization include:

- Knowledge can be collectively and meaningfully organized by people who are, in fact, an extraordinary source of information about the real world they inhabit.

- People can and should create their own future.

- People want opportunities to engage their heads and hearts as well as their hands.

- Cooperation and equality and empowerment help people feel more knowledgeable about and in control of their future.

A well-planned and managed future search conference can be very effective in shaping a learning organization. The new shared vision will undoubtedly impact organizational polices and practices, cause learning to be aligned to organizational goals, and maximize knowledge to improve product and service quality.

2. Gain Top Level Management Support for Becoming a Learning Organization and for Championing Learning Projects

Gain support of top-level management in making the challenge of being a learning organization a part of the vision, structure, strategy, and culture of the company.

Once the company has decided to become a learning organization, it is very important to disseminate this vision and value within and outside the organization, through methods such as announcements, posters, newsletters, videos, symbols, etc. Financial and human resources need to be allocated to make the vision a reality.

Top managers should not only articulate the vision, but be active early participants in its actualization. They should be strong advocates or champions of corporatewide learning efforts. Their modeling of a learning organization is the most powerful way to disseminate the vision and inspire others within the company to join the bandwagon.

3. Create a Corporate Climate for Continuous Learning

For people to actively and enthusiastically participate in the rigors and challenges of a learning organization, a corporate environment that supports and rewards learning must be created. Some ways for developing such a climate are:

- Establish the practice of learning as the key to the organization's purpose and success.
- Create a culture of continuous improvement.
- Support mistakes for the effort and learning gained.
- Share problems and errors; do not hide them.
- Show concern for development of the whole person.
- Expand accessibility of information.
- Help make learning a habit.
- View performance shortfalls as opportunities for learning.

4. Reengineer Policies and Structures Around Learning

Learning organizations work best when policies and boundaries are minimized so that knowledge and ideas can quickly and efficiently move within and outside the organization. Reengineering to increase learning in the organization involves the following actions:

- Cut unnecessary restrictions and procedures.
- Shrink size of working units (e.g., ABB, an organization of over 200,000 employees has self-managed units of no more than 50 people).
- Lessen restrictive control of policies to allow greater flexibility.
- Streamline structures and create a more boundaryless company.
- Reduce hierarchy layers.
- Organize operations by projects.
- Enable department/units to act on own initiatives.
- Root out bureaucracies and silly rules (Royal Bank of Canada has a policy of "rotor-rooting out" such unneeded weeds).

5. Recognize and Reward Individual and Team Learning

One of the most powerful management principles in the world is "That which gets rewarded gets done." And its antithesis is "That which is unrewarded is soon abandoned." Therefore it is vital that an organization identify as many ways as possible to reward individual and, even more importantly, team learning. Rewards should be made for actions that directly or indirectly contribute to organizational learning, such as risk taking, commitment to learning and personal mastery, teamwork, encouraging new experiences and ideas, being a teacher/trainer, and passing lessons learned on to teammates and the broader network.

Rewards can and should be financial when possible. But doesn't learning have to be measurable before it can be financially rewarded? Yes, and surely an individual's or team's learning and the impact of that learning on the bottom line can be as measurable as many of the elements we are often evaluated for during performance appraisal time. The quantity and quality of learning that benefits the company can be seen in terms of new and improved products, services, and relationships as well as documented knowledge acquired, created, stored and/or transferred by individuals and groups.

6. Make Learning a Part of All Policies and Procedures

To systematically transform the company into a learning organization, it is absolutely essential to incorporate learning as an automatic and integrated part of all operations, including production, marketing, managing, finance, human resources, etc.

Examples of policies that demonstrate this incorporation of learning are the following:

- Learning in all projects is captured and transferred.

- Managers are hired or promoted on the basis of their learning and ability to enhance the learning of those around them.

- All employees are responsible for acquiring and transferring information.

- Employees are recruited who possess characteristics of good learners, i.e, desire for personal mastery, persistence and initiative, listening, openness to change.

- All employees are trained in core workplace competencies such as how to learn, creative thinking and problem solving, self-development, and leadership and visioning.

7. Establish Centers of Excellence and Demonstration Projects

A valuable strategy used by many learning organizations is to establish centers of excellence with job rotation in and out of the centers. These centers enable an organization to develop and transfer best practices and know-how throughout the organization. Consider systematic job rotation from many different divisions in and out of the center.

A somewhat related strategy is to encourage the creation of demonstration projects in all parts of the organization. These demonstration projects are locations in which more energy and experimentation can be devoted to test out ideas, policies, procedures, products, or services.

8. Use Measurement of Financial and Nonfinancial Areas as a Learning Activity

Another key principle of management is "That which gets measured gets done." Therefore learning organizations measure not only financial areas—profits, return on investments, expenditures—but areas such as quality and customer satisfaction as they relate to expenditures. Motorola, for example, calculates a 3 to 1 return on each dollar spent on training, and actually seeks to spend as many wise dollars as possible on learning, since it knows that quality will improve the bottom line.

In addition, discourses about metrics—e.g, whether they should be internally or externally focused, the degree of specificity sought, the use of custom-built or standard measures—are all important learning activities. And searching for the most appropriate metrics in itself can be a valuable aspect of learning.

9. Create Time, Space, and Physical Environment for Learning

Organizational learning cannot be pushed too fast. For example, despite a person's natural creativity, there are times when a needed creative idea doesn't emerge immediately. Pushing too hard for innovative ideas may create stress that inhibits, rather than helps, the needed breakthrough.

Although a committed learning group may seek to move quickly to reach the learning destination, it is important to remember there are some inherent speed limits. People need time to plan and reflect; they need physical, social, and mental space to listen and be creative. They need to take the time to listen. Sometimes by slowing down, you find the shorter route to get there faster. In their commitment to provide time for reflecting and learning, some firms have gone so far as to provide 3- to 12-month sabbaticals for staff to visit and work with industry leaders or study at academic centers.

Also the importance of architecture and surroundings (e.g, windows, walls, open spaces, grass and water, art) should be recognized in creating an environment more conducive to learning and to sharing knowledge.

10. Make Learning Intentional at All Times and in All Locations

There are a potpourri of ways to make learning as intentional as possible:

- Encourage success-sharing meetings.
- Practice action learning as much as possible.
- Set aside time at meetings and programs to reflect on learnings.
- Hire or contract with outsiders to bring new ideas to the organization.
- Generate as many explicit learning strategies as possible that fit your organization.

5
Empowering and Enabling People

People are the masters.

EDMUND BURKE

People are the pivotal part of learning organizations because only people, in fact, learn. People are the masters who can take data and transform it into valuable knowledge for personal and organizational use. In our systems learning organization model, the people subsystem includes employees, managers/leaders, customers, suppliers and vendors, alliances, and community (see Figure 5-1).

To be an effective part of organizational learning, these groups of people need to be empowered and enabled. If these groups are empowered but not enabled, they are very dangerous "mad pilots," with lots of power but no direction. If they are enabled but not empowered, they are like "caged eagles," with lots of ability that they are not allowed to use. Let us explore some ways in which each of the groups can be empowered and enabled to be qualified and proficient for organizational learning.

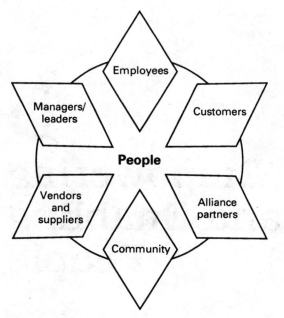

Figure 5-1. People subsystem.

Employees

There are several principles and guidelines to consider in the empowerment and enablement of employees.

Treat Employees as Mature, Capable Workers and Learners

The first thing learning companies do is to treat their employees as adults who have innate capability to learn, who can handle problems, and who enjoy responsibility and recognition. They are also able to elevate their productive, creative learning capacities. Simply put, people should be treated as adults with adult potentialities.

Encourage Employee Freedom, Energy, and Enthusiasm

Learners need to have freedom and support. Enthusiastic and energetic employees are much more creative and committed to learning and productivity. Peter Senge, whose ideas have attracted wide attention on the subject of learning organizations, has described learning organizations as places where people can "continually expand their capacity to create the results they truly desire, where new and expansive patterns of thinking are nurtured, where collective aspiration is set free, and where people are continually learning how to learn together" (*The Fifth Discipline*, p. 3).

Maximize the Delegation of Authority and Responsibility

Learning organizations reduce dependency and increase responsibility as close as possible to the point of action and decision making. The place of power and learning is thus pushed to where the best information and greatest need exist. Operations and power are decentralized and delegated so as to equal the responsibility and learning capacity of the individuals and teams involved.

It is important to realize that accountability and empowerment have not been well correlated in most companies. Too many organizations have made employees accountable but have not empowered them. (Witness the bureaucracies of Eastern Europe and elsewhere.) Empowerment, for Jim Gannon of Royal Bank of Canada, is determined "by the amount of influence, trust, and ability to get exceptions that the employee has."

Involve Employees in Developing Strategies and Planning

In an increasingly dynamic, interdependent, and unpredictable world, it is simply no longer possible for anyone to figure it all out at the top by themselves. The old model of organization leadership—the top thinks and the bottom acts—must now give way to an integration of everyone thinking and acting at all levels at all times. Sharing power with employees makes good business and personal sense. The old days when a Henry Ford, Alfred Sloan, or Tom Watson "learned" for the organization are long and thankfully gone.

Accordingly, employees should be empowered to take part in planning and to develop strategy and tactics in areas that affect their professional work. Learning organizations realize that empowered workers are able to make decisions that are as good as, if not better than, the decisions made by managers because the workers, in fact, possess the best information.

Strike a Balance between Individual and Organization Needs

Learning organizations strike a balance between the development needs of the individual and the organization so that both are properly addressed. There is concern not only for organizational productivity and profits but for the quality of the working lives of employees. Leadership fully recognizes that better organizational results are built upon happy, productive individuals.

Learning organizations seek to develop the full range of human potential and to respect the social and spiritual needs of employees as well as their economic needs. There is a high regard for human dignity and a delight in (not merely tolerance of) ethnic and cultural differences.

Because knowledge demands are growing exponentially, workers often feel overwhelmed by all they need to learn for their jobs. An organizational learning culture can help ease those feelings, since responsibility for learning is shared in such a culture. Also, if the organization supports continuous growth and learning, the possibility of becoming more self-actualized and fulfilled in one's work increases.

Learning organizations are also conscious of the growing pressures on workers to meet family and work obligations, so they try to be *family-friendly* by offering profamily company policies, such as flexible work arrangements, dependent-care services, and wellness programs. Corning and Royal Bank of Canada, for example, have made such programs an integral part of their human resource and learning support policy.

The balance model in Figure 5-2 demonstrates the equilibrium

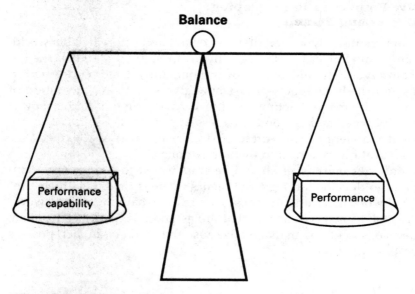

Figure 5-2. Balance model.

HONDA'S SUCCESS IN EMPOWERING AND ENABLING FACTORY-FLOOR EMPLOYEES

There is a saying at Honda that there is "more knowledge on the factory floor than in the office." Therefore, there should be an equal allocation of power to match this high level of commitment, creativity, and intellectual capacity among associates. (All employees at Honda are called *associates*—including the company president.) But Honda does not just talk empowerment, it permits people to set out and actually create a new car. That's empowerment, enablement, and a whole lot more!

Honda managers believe that the associate is the most qualified and best person to know how the job should be done. If managers notice a problem, they solicit the associates for their input, involvement, and advice. The Honda attitude toward the worker-learner is: "We have a goal here. If you can do it better—do it. If you fail, we'll pick you up and dust you off, and encourage you to keep trying."

A key to Honda's success is *gemba*, a Japanese word which means "the place of action," commonly used to mean the shop floor. At Honda, gemba brings together people involved with a particular project or process at the point at which some action needs to happen. This is more than simultaneous engineering and cross-functional teamwork on a project. Rather, it is more like spontaneous action learning.

An example of the power and effectiveness of gemba occurred at the Marysville, Ohio, plant during the development of the Honda wagon. During the initial development process, it was discovered that installing the wiring harness in the tailgate required 10 minutes, which was too long a time period. All the Honda people involved— design engineers, assemblers, and people from stamping—arrived on the scene where the prototype was being built. It was up to them to make the changes needed to get the harness installed quickly and efficiently. Decisions could be, and were, made. The solution was quickly discovered (it involved switching to a two-piece wiring harness and increasing the diameter of the hole through which the wiring was fed).

Employee power and ability are terms used often by the people at Honda. There are also expressions of confidence, responsibility, pride, and most important, accomplishment. Robert Simcox, plant manager at the Marysville assembly plant, says that Honda people are learning together and are successful because "They have been given the opportunity to use their own creativity and imagination."

between the needs of the individual and those of the organization. To enhance performance, the organization must continually build the performance capabilities of the individual and hence the organization. Performance and performance capability should therefore be viewed as two separate but integrated dimensions ideally in balance.

Managers/Leaders

Many leadership styles that were acceptable in the past will be unacceptable in the learning organization of the future. Hard-nosed managers who single-handedly and forcefully determined team direction, made key decisions, and pushed employees may prove destructive in today's organizations. Such managers will not be welcome in the organization that has been transformed from steady-state control to learning, empowerment, and continuous change (see Figure 5-3).

Managers will need to move from controlling to empowering, from being a commander to being a steward, from acting as a transitional manager to acting as a transformational leader. The new organization requires a new type of leader possessing new kinds of roles and skills.

New Leadership Roles

Let's explore the many new roles required of manager in a learning organization:

Instructor, Coach, and Mentor. The most important responsibility for a manager in organizations today is to enable people around him or

From	To
Continual change	Transformation
Quality improvement	Process engineering
Matrix	Network
Performance appraisal	Performance management
Technophobia	Application of technology
Functions	Process
Control	Empowerment
Employment	Employability

Figure 5-3. Changes in organizations.

Dimension	Instructor	Coach	Mentor
Focus of help	Task	Results of job	Development of person throughout life
Timespan	Day or two	Month or year	Career or lifetime
Approach to helping	Show and tell; give supervised; practice; set up opportunities to try out new skills	Explore problem together	Act as friend; listen and question to enlarge awareness
Associated activities	Analyze task; give clear instructions; supervise practice; give feedback on results at once	Jointly identify the problem; create development opportunities and review	Link work with other parts of life; clarify broad and long-term aims and purpose in life
Ownership	Helper	Shared	Learner

Figure 5-4. The manager facilitates learning.

her to learn. Helping others learn will require a variety of approaches; the manager will have to be an instructor, a coach, and a mentor. The type of role will depend on the focus of help needed, the timespan of the learning, the approach to learning, the activities involved, and the ownership of the learning, as shown in Figure 5-4.

Knowledge Manager. The learning organization will consist of knowledge specialists who will be colleagues and associates of equal rank. No knowledge area will necessarily rank higher than another; each will be judged by its contribution to the success of the learning organization. This information-based, egalitarian company will need a leader who can motivate and assist colleagues in the collection, storage, and distribution of knowledge within and outside the unit. He or she will help determine what knowledge is important for organizational memory, assure that mechanisms exist for gathering and coding the knowledge, and encourage people to transfer and use knowledge.

Colearner and Model for Learning. The leaders will not just tell others what to learn. They will encourage, motivate, and help workers to learn and to continuously improve their skills as well as their learning abilities. Leaders will assist workers in identifying learning resources. Leaders will be devoted learners who take time to learn and demonstrate a love for learning. Practicing action learning, taking risks, seeking innovative answers, and asking fresh questions all exhibit solid learning practices and skills to employees.

Architect and Designer. With the new technologies, structures, environment, and resources of a learning organization, the leader must be an architect who can "fit" or "sculpt" these elements into a system which will thrive in the rapidly changing marketplace. The leader helps to redefine the organization, reshape the networks and teams, and reinvent new methods for selecting, training, and rewarding people so that everyone can participate in the new global environment. The leader must also help create and design new and appropriate policies, strategies, and principles.

Coordinator. Similar to the conductor of an orchestra who enables each orchestra player to play his instrument more magnificently, the learning leader coordinates and empowers many people to perform their best. The leader utilizes a repertoire of approaches and styles to track information, polish products and services, and energize people from within and outside the organization.

Another analogy might be that of a coach of a soccer team who transforms individuals into a cohesive unit in which every member is responsible for the success of the team and can see how his or her play affects the whole game. The manager motivates, implores, inspires, and promotes every team member.

Advocate and Champion for Learning Processes and Projects.
Robust organizational learning requires more than one advocate or champion if it is to succeed. This is particularly true in the case of learning that is related to changing a basic value or a long-cherished approach. The greater the number of advocates who promote a new learning idea or program, the more rapidly and extensively will organizationwide learning take place. Although it ought to be possible for any person to be an advocate for learning processes and projects, the manager is often the best and most likely source; he or she should welcome, if not solicit, the opportunity to be a learning champion.

New Leadership Skills

In addition to the new leadership roles for managers in learning organizations, there are several new skills required by managers.

Build a Shared Vision. The learning leader must envision together with his or her fellow employees the type of future world the company desires, one that is exciting and challenging enough to attract and retain the best and brightest of know-how workers. To the extent that the manager is truly able to build a shared, desired picture for the organization or unit, to that extent staff are willing and committed to carry out the vision. Leaders should attempt to:

- Blend extrinsic and intrinsic visions
- Communicate their own vision and ask for support
- Encourage personal visions from which emerge shared visions
- Keep visioning as an ongoing process

Coordinate Multiple, Task-Focused Teams. In the changing organization with its increased use of project teams, managers will very likely be leading and coordinating 3, 5, even up to 10 different task-focused teams, each carrying out a variety of activities on totally different time schedules. The ability to quickly enter into and become a trusted partner of these teams is a taxing challenge. To plan, manage, balance, and juggle these many "balls" requires an agile, caring, and well-organized individual.

Surface and Test Mental Models. Many of the best ideas of an organization never get put into practice because they often conflict with existing, established, mental models or ways of doing things. The new leader has the task of confronting these existing assumptions without invoking defensiveness or anger. Specific skills in this area include:

- Balancing inquiry and advocacy
- Distinguishing between what is espoused from what is practiced
- Recognizing and defusing defensive routines
- Seeing and testing leaps of abstraction

Engage in Systems Thinking. Leaders in learning organizations must help people see the big picture, with the underlying trends, forces, and potential surprises. They need to think systematically and be able to foresee how internal and external factors might benefit or destroy the organization. The ability to decipher and analyze massive amounts of sometimes contradictory information demands patience and persistence. Some key talents needed to accomplish this include:

- Avoiding symptomatic solutions and focusing on underlying causes
- Distinguishing detail complexity (many variables) from dynamic

complexity (when cause and effect are distant in time and space, and when the consequences over time are subtle)

- Seeing processes, not snapshots
- Focusing on areas of high leverage
- Seeing interrelationships, not things
- Seeing that you and the cause of your problems are part of a single system

Encourage Creativity, Innovation, and Willingness to Risk. Jack Welch, CEO of General Electric, challenges his managers with the following questions: Are you dealing with new things? Are you coming up with fundamentally new approaches for getting things done? Are you generating new programs?

For General Electric and other learning companies, the generation of new ideas is the lifeline to continued success. Although everyone is encouraged and expected to be creative, it is the managers who can best create an environment that encourages risk taking and at the same time protects and supports those whose risks have not been successful. Managers can be leaders in attempting new things and challenging the old ways.

Conceptualize and Inspire Learning and Action. The ability to conceptualize complex issues and processes, simplify them, and inspire people around them are necessary competencies of the transformational leader. Charisma may be helpful, but it is much more important to lead through a caring confidence in the people for whom you are a "steward." Gaining workers' participation in challenging, sometimes unenjoyable activities requires solid facilitating and coordinating skills. And no task is more important than encouraging and inspiring learning!

Customers

Learning organizations know that because customers can be a fertile source of information and ideas, they should be closely linked into the learning system and strategy of the organization.

Conversations and information gathering from customers invariably provide new knowledge for the company for customers, after all, have expertise in what they do or buy. Customers can provide up-to-date product information, competitive comparisons, insights into changing preferences, and immediate feedback about service and patterns of use. Learning organizations should therefore:

1. Provide ongoing, accessible training and learning opportunities (e.g., video training, embedded technology, classroom instruction) to educate the customer about their products. This not only creates an informed customer who can provide better ideas and insights on how to improve the product or service, but also cultivates greater loyalty from a fellow learner and partner. Both the Dana Corporation and Ford Truck, for example, offer courses to help improve the business performance of their customers, such as how to generate repeat business (Dana) and consultative selling skills (Ford).

2. Encourage and support the customer's expectations of improved quality, new innovations, and quicker speed since this will serve as an incentive to constantly improve and therefore learn. Milliken's staff, for example, accompanies the first shipment of all the company's products in order to see how they are used; they are then better able to develop ideas for further improvement of those products.

3. Actively seek feedback, suggestions, and consultation with customers and suppliers. Senior executives of Motorola, including the CEO, meet personally and on a regular basis with customers. Worthington Steel machine operators make periodic trips to customers' factories to discover their needs.

Suppliers and Vendors

Learning organizations realize that success is dependent to a large extent upon the success of the company's entire business network, not just its employees and customers, but also suppliers and vendors. Having others in the business chain collectively learn about commitments and policies as well as appropriate management or technical skills can be very valuable to everyone's long-range fortunes. Learning resources and courses available for staff can be made available to the company's important, long-term partners. Rover, the highly successful British automobile manufacturer, provides numerous learning opportunities for its dealers in areas of quality, leadership, and staff development.

Alliances

The growing presence of global competition and virtual organizations have drastically increased the number of short-term alliances formed between and among companies. Most companies use the alliance for the purpose of increasing profits and market share or for cutting expenses, time, duplication, and politics.

Learning organizations, however, seek to add another very important, long-term benefit to the alliance—learning. Up front, at the very beginning of the relationship, the learning company considers the possible learnings from the alliance: customer intelligence, process and operations policies, cultural nuances, etc. They may even build these learning objectives into the agreement. Learning companies then provide an adequate exchange of personnel to be sure to capture and bring the learning back. The short-term alliance provides valuable learning and therefore becomes a rich, long-term investment and profit that can be leveraged for future successes.

Community

Learning organizations recognize that many benefits accrue by involving the community as a part of the learning process, such as: (1) the enhancement of the company's image in the community, (2) the generation of greater community interest in working for or buying from the company, (3) strengthening of the quality of life in the community, (4) the preparation of a future workforce, and (5) the opportunity to exchange and share community resources.

National Semiconductor, located in Santa Clara, California, has actively involved the community in its organization learning efforts. The company runs numerous programs for local schools, superintendents of the county schools, high school teachers, and elementary school science teachers. In being a good community member, National Semiconductor learns and gains as well. Entering into a new market early can build a good community image for the company. By establishing a branch of National Semiconductor University to train the upcoming workforce in the school system, National is preparing future engineers for semiconductor technology. In this way, according to Kevin Wheeler, Director of National Semiconductor University, "We have a trained workforce ready, willing and able to work for National. The community benefits by learning about technology, electronics, and American management styles. And National benefits by learning a lot about the local culture and needs of people in that culture."

Conclusion

The demarcations between management and employees, between departments and units, between employees and customers, between the company and its vendors, and even between the company and its competitors have become less permanent and more flexible.

Empowering and enabling these various groups of people extends and strengthens the learning enterprise.

Corporate Leader in People Empowerment Subsystem— Whirlpool

Founded in 1911 in Benton Harbor, Michigan, Whirlpool Corporation is the world's leading manufacturer and marketer of major home appliances. The company manufactures in 11 countries and markets products in more than 140 countries under brand names such as Whirlpool, KitchenAid, Roper, Estate, Bajknecht, Ignis, Laden, and Inglis. Whirlpool has over 40,000 employees worldwide. 1994 revenues exceeded $8 billion.

For the past several years, Whirlpool has been pursuing a strategy of international growth, purchasing part of Philips in Europe in 1989, SAGAD of Argentina in 1992, and Kelvinator of India in 1994. For a long time number one in the United States and Canada, Whirlpool is now the third largest appliance marketer in Europe and number one in Latin America. And with sales in Asia expected to grow three to four times faster than in the United States in the next few years, Whirlpool has stepped up its operations there, setting up a regional office in Singapore in 1993.

Whirlpool has become a global leader not only in home appliances, but also in corporatewide learning. Corporate analysts attribute much of Whirlpool's success to its global vision and global strategy, areas in which *Business Week* declares, "They are outpacing the industry dramatically" (November 28, 1994, p. 98). The beginnings of this vision and strategies to accomplish it emerged as a result of a brilliantly designed global planning conference in Switzerland in 1990.

Using Action Learning and Empowered People to Become a Global Company

In 1989, Whirlpool acquired the $2 billion appliance division of Philips, headquartered in the Netherlands. In one fell swoop, Whirlpool had gone from an almost exclusively domestic company to a 40 percent global corporation, and in the process, had become the largest household appliances company in the world.

The significance of becoming a global company was quickly seen by Whirlpool. Impressive amounts of learning would be needed if the company was to successfully adapt and transform itself to compete for customers in the new global environment. And Whirlpool had a far distance to go—many of its U.S. senior managers didn't even have passports. Integrating the American and Dutch companies would not be easy.

CEO Dave Whitwam asked the human resources staff to develop policies and programs to help the company globalize. Within six months of the acquisition, Whirlpool brought 150 of its senior managers from 16 countries to Montreux, Switzerland, for a one-week global conference. The theme of the conference was "Winning Through Quality Leadership: One Global Vision." Four major goals were identified for the conference:

- Advance a unified vision of the company's future.

- Instill the idea of embracing the future as one global company.

- Establish a keen sense of responsibility within the leadership group for creating the company's future.

- Identify and initiate explicit steps toward integrating various activities and ideas throughout Whirlpool's worldwide operations into a unified whole.

Encouraging cultural mixing between the 150 managers was deemed crucial for action learning to take place. The typical behavior of international managers gravitating toward their own "cultural cocoons" was avoided by planning activities and events that pushed managers beyond their own national backgrounds and people of their own language.

The well-planned structure of the conference freed the managers to be creative, reflective, and open to new possibilities. Emphasis was on meeting, getting to know and trust, working with, and learning with their new global colleagues. Together, they could better focus on critical, challenging issues such as the Whirlpool vision, strategic planning, and quality.

One element which built powerful learning among the global participants was the conference ground rules. Attendees were encouraged to be active themselves, and to help others participate as well, in both the meetings and informal activities. They were challenged to get beyond their comfort zones with these guidelines:

- Create situations in which you can meet everyone.

- Promote an atmosphere of worldwide learning. Remember that the only problems we cannot solve are the ones we don't identify.

- We are all responsible for making the week productive.
- Be a good listener.

Whirlpool managers themselves prepared and conducted the various workshops. This tactic began the process that continues today of managers of the new Whirlpool being learning facilitators and trainers as well as managers.

During the weeklong event, managers were invited to identify which major areas of the company's operations could be improved. From an original list of 200 areas, 15 key issue were identified. Each of these issues became Whirlpool's One-Company Challenges. The challenges ranged from global management reporting systems to global quality initiatives, from development of a global corporate talent pool to consumer-product delivery cycles.

Fifteen cross-functional and multinational groups, called Whirlpool One-Company Challenge Teams were then formed to examine these 15 topics and present their recommendations at the following global conference in Washington, D.C. Team members met regularly and reported their progress in *The Leading Edge*, the corporate newsletter for Whirlpool's worldwide leaders.

Listen to how Whitwam describes the role of Whirlpool staff in developing and implementing the new company vision: "We made those 150 people accountable for educating all of our 38,000 people around the world. When going global, you have to communicate to everyone what the company vision is and what the long-term goals are. And then you have to follow through and design processes that force the interaction to continue. Every single employee must believe that there is great value in managing the company in an integrated way. To do that, you have to bring people together on real projects that tackle real problems or that explore opportunities on a cross-border basis."

The learning and change that this global conference achieved was so significant that Whirlpool people felt it launched the company ahead in time by three to five years in the integration of its global management team, and also saved the company millions of dollars in the process. It was at this conference that the vision of a global learning company and the values of "commitment to people," all people, began to emerge.

Commitment to People

One of Whirlpool's greatest achievements as a company has been its commitment to people—to its 40,000 employees and managers, its mil-

WHIRLPOOL VALUES STATEMENT

We, the people of Whirlpool, aren't "in" the company; we "are" the company. As such, we recognize our individual responsibility to assure our collective success by practicing and promoting the following values.

Business with Integrity

We will pursue our business with honor, fairness and respect for both the individual and the public at large...ever mindful that there is no right way to do a wrong thing.

Quality as a Quest

Success depends on our ability to deliver a level of excellence respected by all who rely on us. We will lift the quality and value of our products and services above the expectations of those who receive them...always recognizing that our best today can be bettered tomorrow.

Customers as the Focus

We will dedicate ourselves to anticipate the changing needs of customers and to create innovative and superior products and services, faster and more effectively than our competitors.

Commitment to the Common Good

We will serve responsibly as members of all communities in which we live and work, respecting cultural distinctions throughout the world. We will preserve the environment, prudently utilize natural resources and maintain all property we are privileged to use.

Power of Trust

A mutual and inspiring trust, nurtured by honest and open communication and equal opportunity, should unite our actions and relationships with one another...providing a foundation for teamwork, confidence and loyalty.

Learning to Lead

Our competitive edge in the marketplace ultimately depends on how our skills and expertise measure against the world's best. To lead the best, we must cultivate our talents through continuous training...confident that we will be provided every opportunity to widen our horizons.

Spirit of Winning

At the heart of the company values lies company spirit. It encompasses the determination, resourcefulness, boldness and vigor by which we work. Collectively, we believe this urgent and relentless drive will enable us to shape the future of our industry...and deliver the performance that earns us success in the marketplace.

lions of customers, its numerous partners, and to the global community at large. This commitment to developing and caring for all the people inside and outside the company and helping them learn can be clearly seen by viewing Whirlpool's values statement.

Whirlpool hires and develops employees who possess the following five attributes, all of which are essential characteristics of the learning employee and contribute toward building a learning organization:

1. Integrity: to behave honestly

2. Commitment: to express one's full potential capability and energy at work

3. Reliability: to be counted on consistently to do what is expected or required

4. Initiative: to originate new ideas or methods without being asked

5. Cooperativeness: to work together with others toward a common purpose

Commitment to Quality Learning for All Employees

Whirlpool believes that it cannot expect continuous improvement in its key business processes without investing in the education and training of all its people at all levels on a systematic basis. A manifestation of this pledge is Whirlpool's just completed state-of-the-art, $5.5 million Corporate Development Center near corporate headquarters in Brandywine Creek, Michigan.

Tom Helton, Director of human resources and driving force behind its development, describes the center as a most critical "vehicle to help further the business agenda of the corporation and carry out our company's strategic design. Through this construction, Whirlpool has demonstrated its commitment to the lifelong learning of its employees."

The 56,000-square-foot building features video and broadcast systems, breakout rooms, and an amphitheater with computerized projection screen. The proximity to Whirlpool administration center allows Whirlpool executives to come to the center to teach classes, half of which are taught by the headquarters leadership. Helton praises the involvement of top-level managers in guiding the learning process. "It sends a tremendous message about the importance of learning to participants when they see the CEO of a company teaching."

The major mission of the corporate center is to provide Whirlpool with:

- A visible focal point from which to drive a single, integrated training and education agenda, worldwide
- Professionally competent leaders of character to serve the company's customers, shareholders, and other stakeholders
- Highly effective individuals, teams, and organizations capable of winning in every region, country, and market in the world.

Inherent in this mission are three overarching goals: (1) develop a global mindset, (2) align the organization with Whirlpool's vision, strategic design, and business strategies, and (3) build the knowledge and skill necessary to win.

Whirlpool's learning programs, according to Helton, contain a "bold, new strategy," one which embodies consistency of application, impact in the organization, and speed in execution. Acquiring, leveraging, and transferring knowledge, skills, capabilities, and best practices will be critical for corporatewide learning.

Two of the major programs at the corporate center are:

1. *The Whirlpool Leadership Academy*, with a core curriculum of leadership-oriented courses, provides the knowledge and skills necessary to develop and strengthen leadership capabilities.

2. *The Whirlpool Excellence Academy* is designed to support Whirlpool excellence system and other Whirlpool business strategies by enabling people to acquire, improve, and maintain their job-related knowledge and skills.

Empowering Whirlpool's People

Whirlpool has set a high standard of commitment to its employees called *high-performance partnership*. It represents a promise to all of Whirlpool's people that the company will encourage and enable contribution and commitment from each individual and team, and will provide a dynamic and diverse workplace environment which is valued by all. Whirlpool has set a clearly defined goal of achieving a corporate people commitment index of 85 (on a scale of 100), which represents a high level of company and employee commitment to each other.

People commitment, for Whirlpool, means:

- Living the shared values in the workplace
- Recognizing and rewarding performance
- Training and educating
- Listening to concerns and ideas
- Contributing and sharing ideas

As CEO Dave Whitwam recently wrote, "One of the approaches we're using to help employees feel like owners is to give them responsibility. We need their heads thinking as well as their hands working. In some of our factories today, there is no supervisor on the floor. Teams made up of hourly workers hire new employees, create production line layouts, decide on production levels, and even make employee termination recommendations. They drive the quality process. That's a real change from how industrial companies have traditionally been managed."

Another way in which Whirlpool has demonstrated it commitment to empowering and enabling employees is through its compensation system, which is driven by the principle of pay for performance. Essentially all of Whirlpool employees received stock options in 1991. Some operations provide gain-sharing programs that allow employees to benefit directly from their own productivity and quality improvements. Being stockholders as well as stakeholders has provided even more incentive for workers to become active learners, since they can directly benefit when they tackle and solve company problems.

Whitwam goes on to say in the company's latest annual report that "the commitment and effort of the 40,000 people we employ worldwide were crucial to our performance this past year, and we have many programs in place to further encourage going forward. Whirlpool Excellence Systems (WES) has helped our men and women understand the need to make decisions and carry out their jobs for the purpose of satisfying customers—and to challenge those decisions that they believe fall short of the mark. So, too, have innovative performance-based compensation system at all levels within the corporations. Whirlpool has made substantial progress toward becoming an integrated global home-appliance company, one in which its people share the best of what they know and do with colleagues worldwide."

Whirlpool seeks to tap the creativity and skills of its enabled employees around the world to provide quality and competitive prices for its customers in all markets. Cost and quality improvements, higher customer satisfaction, and greater efficiencies, resulting from the sharing of best practices in areas including product development, engineering, procurement, manufacturing, marketing, sales, and distribution, contribute to Whirlpool's strong global performance.

Importance of Measurement for Learning

Whirlpool is an example of a learning organization that carefully measures nonfinancial as well as financial factors. In 1991, CEO David Whitwam announced that the four value-creating objectives of the organization (i.e., cost, quality, productivity, and customer satisfaction) would be publicly announced and measured on an annual basis. The ongoing measuring of these objectives, Whitwam stated, "would become a powerful tool" in maintaining the learning power of Whirlpool.

The building of Whirlpool's measurement system began by benchmarking companies such as Nestle, Fiat, Hitachi, and Mitsubishi so as to obtain appropriate measurements for world-class performance. "Unless you put visible measures in place that you can quantify, it is very hard for people to manage them," according to Ralph Hake, then corporate controller for Whirlpool.

Nonfinancial measures are now analyzed at bimonthly board meetings not only to examine results but to identify correlations between financial and nonfinancial factors. There is a high focus on identifying areas for improvement as well as ongoing development of the measurement tools. Hake proclaims that "Whirlpool has significantly improved its learning and its performance" as a result of using nonfinancial measures. Board member Robert Burnett, retired chairman and CEO of Meredith Corporation and a member of several other boards, says that relative to measurement, Whirlpool is "doing a better job than anyone else in the industry."

Action Learning, Leadership, and Customers

At Whirlpool, line managers run action learning groups composed of frontline workers. Helton proudly notes, "We have close to 100 percent of our line mangers actually conducting the action training. The role of training and human resource people has become largely one of training line mangers to be trainers."

Whirlpool is dedicated to building a perfect product for the customer. With that as the point of departure, you can indeed take the notion of satisfying the customer to a completely different plane, and that's where breakthrough learning has become possible for Whirlpool.

In the most recent annual report, employees from around the world were cited for how their knowledge and initiative led to significant benefits for Whirlpool customers. Here are some examples:

- A cross-functional team developed Whirlpool's award-winning superefficient refrigerator
- A learning group devised a just-in-time system to supply product kits and components
- A project team leveraged knowledge from North America into a new dryer designed for European customers.
- Cross-functional employee groups in Europe refined complex manufacturing processes

Empowering Customers

To gain this ability to delight the customer, Whirlpool has emphasized to its people the importance of learning from the customer. Success, according to Whitwam, means understanding better than anyone in the industry the present and future needs of consumers and trade partners. Whirlpool believes that its research in these areas is the most exhaustive in the home-appliance industry.

By paying consumers to "play around" with appliances at its Usability Lab in Comerio, Italy, Whirlpool discovered that microwave oven sales would improve if it introduced a model that browned food. The result: Whirlpool developed the VIP Crisp. Now, it's Europe's best-seller, and Whirlpool recently began making it in the United States.

Whirlpool recognizes that doing business successfully in a geographic region requires a thorough understanding of consumers and the market as a whole. In Asia, for example, Whirlpool recently conducted focus group sessions with 1000 consumers in nine countries, surveys among 6500 households, 700 consumer discussions in four countries, and other extensive research through economic, diplomatic, and regulatory sources. Whirlpool has also benchmarked other Western companies that have been successful in the Asia region, among them, Motorola, Procter & Gamble, AT&T, Emerson, Westinghouse, Hewlett-Packard, and McDonald's.

Learning with and from Partners

Whirlpool has also developed close learning relationships with organizations in related businesses, such as Procter & Gamble and Unilever. In these and other partnerships there are not only exchanges of basic information and ideas, but also more intensive involvements at the development, engineering, and technology levels.

As Whirlpool enters into the People's Republic of China (PRC), it is prepared to share its expertise in technology, manufacturing, human resources management, innovative product designs, and such modern infrastructure support as information technology. Overall, the potential for long-term links between Whirlpool and PRC are enormous and mutually beneficial.

As a world leader in establishing trade partnerships, Whirlpool has strategic agreements with three of the top four major domestic retailers in North America, three of the top five in Europe, and most leading retailers in South America. These partnerships have produced significant learnings and driven Whirlpool's business success.

Whirlpool, as a result of its learning prowess, is making great strides in reaching its goal of being a leader in the ever-changing global environment. Whirlpool people know that the company's vision of reaching worldwide to bring excellence home depends on their ability to provide continuous quality improvement and to exceed customers' expectations. They know that they will gain competitive advantage through this and by building on existing strengths and developing new competencies.

As an emerging learning organization, this vision and those capabilities are becoming more and more of a reality each and every day. Whitwam and the people of Whirlpool have wisely recognized that continuous change is the essence of the global market and only by empowering and enabling people from throughout the organization and across the business chain can they successfully lead in this global market.

Ten Top Strategies for People Empowerment and Enablement in Learning Organizations

1. Institute Personnel Policies That Reward Learners

Many organizations do not follow through on their stated values of recruiting and rewarding people who are learners. In learning organizations, however, people who learn and help people around them to learn are promoted, rewarded financially, and given better career opportunities. The company looks for potential leaders from among staff who take advantage of learning opportunities, who ask fresh questions so as to optimize learning from experience, and who learn well in team settings.

On the other hand, nonlearners, people who are afraid to take risks, who do not value acquiring and transferring knowledge, are encouraged to seek opportunities outside the organization.

2. Create Self-Managed Work Teams

Probably the most direct way for an organization to demonstrate that it has confidence in the level of empowerment and enablement of its employees is through the use of self-managed work teams (also referred to as self-directed work teams or high-involvement teams). Several learning organizations—Saturn, Hewlett-Packard, General Electric—have had great success with self-managed work teams.

A number of important principles must be understood and put into place so as to build and support such teams. There should be:

- Clear goals and an understanding of what power or decision-making authority the team has
- A clear timeframe
- Strong intergroup skills
- Understanding of group processes and functions
- Group procedures for working within the team and communicating outside the team
- Compatibility of team-based management with the organization's policies, procedures, and systems
- Confidence in the group so as not to overreact to a team's mistakes or slowness
- Flexibility in allowing a work team to push beyond its original boundaries

3. Empower Employees to Learn and Produce

Oftentimes *empowerment* is only a slogan used by top management; The concept is not practiced, particularly when important planning decisions are to be made. Employees quickly grasp this distinction and put less energy and creativity into implementing company operations. The brainpower of the organization is barely tapped.

Learning organizations, however, empower and "informate" their workers with knowledge about financial, technical, and other data so that they can make wiser decisions. They then entrust them with the courage and responsibility of being successful.

Truly empowering organizations realize that it is essential to push responsibility as close as possible to the action points. They involve employees in planning, evaluating, and determining responsibilities and profits.

A good corporate example of employee empowerment is Saturn, a division of General Motors. The Saturn factory in Spring Hill, Tennessee, was actually conceived by General Motors to be a laboratory for the development of innovative ideas. And one of the most revolutionary ideas is Saturn's approach to employee empowerment. Each Saturn work team manages everything without direct oversight from top management. This includes its own budget, inventory control, and hiring. An example is the Saturn machine maintenance team. It can order many tools and parts it needs on its own, and even choose the outside supplier for transmission components.

This empowerment helps the employees to make better, faster decisions than their office-bound managers. The added responsibility has also made workers more accountable, with absenteeism at 2.5 percent, much less than the 10 to 15 percent at other GM plants. And Saturn, since its conception, has been GM's most successful and innovative division.

4. Encourage Leaders to Model and Demonstrate Learning

Since action usually speaks louder than words, managers should demonstrate by their attitude and their behavior that they appreciate and love learning. They should spend time reading, listening, reflecting, studying, and attending learning programs. Managers should develop and practice the important leadership skills of visioning, mental modeling, and systems thinking. They must recognize that control may make you feel "high," but is a "low" for team and organizational learning.

Leaders should learn from employees and take their ideas seriously. Don't filter out bad news; rather be open to data about the organization, the industry, markets, competition, and customers. Channel information to the appropriate employees without a managerial spin. Develop networks of learners and leaders from learning organizations.

Acknowledge and be open to mistakes made by yourself and others. See these as opportunities for learning.

5. Invite Leaders to Champion Learning Processes and Projects

The primary responsibility of managers in a learning organization is to create and foster a climate that promotes learning. Here are some of the ways that a manager can create such an environment:

- Encourage unsolicited problem-solving ideas.
- Respond to employee ideas and suggestions in a timely way.
- Support those you have empowered.
- Foster partnership and/or teaming with you.
- Commit to allowing airing of differences and working through conflicts.
- Advocate and reward learning.
- Encourage experimentation and reflection on what was learned so that new knowledge can be built.
- Publicly and often talk about learning.
- Generate and enhance learning opportunities wherever and whenever possible.
- Listen to your staff but don't always give answers; encourage them to find the answer themselves.
- Avoid teaching and controlling.
- Slow down, encourage reflection.

6. Balance Learning and Development Needs of the Individual and Organization

Learning organizations must continually build the performance capability of both the individual and the organization. It is important not to allow organizational requirements to overwhelm the personal and performance capability of the individual.

In respecting the whole person—personally, physically, spiritually, socially and economically—as well as his and her family needs, a learning organization tries to be humane and family-friendly. Wellness and physical fitness programs, counselling services, flexible work arrangements, dependent care services, all these allow and enable the worker to better focus energies in being a better learner and a more productive worker.

7. Encourage and Enhance Customer Participation in Organization Learning

Customers are a vital source of information as well as a tremendous impetus to quality and continuous improvement. Learning companies therefore actively share information with customers to obtain their ideas and inputs, and thereby learn how to continuously improve services and products. Encourage the customer to be a part of your learning organization. As fellow team members, they can help identify needs and inadequacies, offer recommendations, and ensure quality.

In order to maximize their involvement in learning and knowledge exchange, it is necessary to provide opportunities for customers to learn about your products, services, vision, collaboration options, etc. Banks can provide information about different types of loans and investments. Zoos can educate the public about the environment as well as the care and feeding of the animals. Computer companies can used embedded technology to train as well as learn from the customers.

Learning exchanges such as these not only augment the learning resources of the organization in the long term, but also build customer loyalty and profits in the short term.

8. Provide Education Opportunities for Community

The communities in which organizations operate represent important sources for present and future learnings, employees, and customers. Learning organizations might consider some of the following community education efforts:

- Allowing teachers, community workers, homemakers, etc., to participate in corporate training programs
- Tutoring or coteaching in the classroom
- Jointly sponsoring learning events with other corporations, academic institutions, or agencies.

9. Build Long-Term Learning Partnerships with Vendors and Suppliers

The agencies and agents that are part of the company's business chain present resources for new ideas, information, and programs as well as opportunities of experimenting with programs or services that may not be attempted within the company itself for financial, political, or human resource reasons.

The purchasing of educational resources, contracting of expertise, and renting of facilities can oftentimes become not only feasible but also much more cost-effective when done with partners. Reflecting with partners on experiences and possibilities can also add to the learning for everyone.

10. Maximize Learning from Alliances and Joint Ventures

For most American firms, an alliance with another company primarily represents an opportunity for increased profits and greater market share over a limited period of time. Learning companies, however, see a much greater long-term benefit of the joint partnership; i.e., the opportunity of acquiring valuable learning. Therefore, they undertake the following actions to maximize their learnings with these short-term business partners:

- Make up-front considerations of what can be learned from alliance; e.g., what the company might learn, what core skills it may be able to build during the alliance, how to best build these skills.

- Build learning objectives into the agreement with responsibilities for learning specified.

- Involve human resources staff to facilitate learning.

- Arrange for exchange of personnel to bring back learning.

6

Knowledge Management in Learning Organizations

Knowledge is power.

FRANCIS BACON

Simply put, knowledge has become more important for organizations than financial resources, market position, technology, or any other company asset. Knowledge is seen as the main resource used in performing work in an organization. The organization's traditions, culture, technology, operations, systems, and procedures are all based on knowledge and expertise.

Employees need knowledge to increase their abilities to improve products and services, thereby providing quality service to clients and consumers. Knowledge is necessary to update products and services as well as to change systems and structures and to communicate solutions to problems.

Knowledge is the food of the learning organization. It is the nutrient

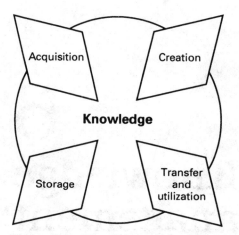

Figure 6-1. Knowledge subsystem.

that enables the organizational to grow. Individuals may come and go, but valuable knowledge cannot be lost or the company starves to death.

In the knowledge subsystem addressed in this chapter, we will look at how knowledge is managed, i.e., how it is acquired, created, stored, and transferred so that it can be utilized and applied (see Figure 6-1).

For organizations to learn effectively and efficiently, the process in the knowledge subsystem must be ongoing and interactive; they should not be seen as being either sequential or independent. The distribution of information should occur through multiple channels, each having different time frames. Moreover, information within the organization should be continually subjected to perceptual filters. Knowledge management requires both a proactive and reactive mode.

Successful learning organizations systematically guide knowledge through all four of the steps in the subsystem so that it can be successfully applied and utilized. The management of knowledge is at the heart of what is organizational learning. Let's enter into the vital nucleus of what learning organizations are all about, the building and using of knowledge.

Knowledge Acquisition

Organizations can acquire knowledge from both external and internal sources.

External Collection of Knowledge

The pace of change is so rapid today that no single organization can ever gain control of or dominate all effective operating practices and good ideas. To be a marketplace leader, an organization must look outward for constant improvement and new ideas. The old school of thought, which held that "If it isn't invented here, it can't be any good," is a curse in today's high-velocity markets. Learning organizations don't need to invent what others have learned to do well. Today's rallying cry for learning companies is "Acquire, adapt, and advance!"

Companies can acquire information from the external environment through a large number of methods:

- Benchmarking from other organizations
- Attending conferences
- Hiring consultants
- Reading print materials such as newspapers, E-mail, and journals
- Viewing television, video, and film
- Monitoring economic, social, and technological trends
- Collecting data from customers, competitors, and resources
- Hiring new staff
- Collaborating with other organizations, building alliances, and forming joint ventures

Benchmarking is rapidly becoming one of the most used and most effective tools for acquiring knowledge. Benchmarking teams are generally mandated to look far and wide for better operating practices. They are the best sentinels that a company can post along the watchtowers of the organization. They can sound the alarm when the first sign appears that the organization has fallen behind the competition or failed to take advantage of important operating improvements developed elsewhere.

Best-practices benchmarking provides an organization with the tools, the rationale, and the process to accept change as constant, inevitable, and good. The ongoing adaptation of best practices helps an organization avoid being ambushed by unexpected change. A company can accelerate its rate of improvement by systematically studying others and by comparing its operations and performance with the best practices of highly innovative and successful companies.

The search for best practices quickly draws a company outside the confines of its own culture and personal habits. Best-practices bench-marking is therefore a pragmatic approach to managing change and performance improvement.

Tomorrow's best practices will inevitably evolve beyond or diverge from today's best practices. By their nature, best practices are dynamic and progressive. For this reason, best-practices benchmarking is often called an *evergreen* process: it renews the organization each time it is repeated. It should be, therefore, an ongoing business process that integrates fully with continuous improvement in an organization.

Benchmarking may be process-oriented (focusing on discrete work processes and operating systems), performance-oriented (focusing on enabling managers to assess their competitive positions through product and service comparisons), or strategically oriented (seeking to identify the winning strategies that have enabled high-performing companies to enjoy success in their marketplaces). It can help an organization with:

- Setting and refining strategy
- Reengineering work processes and business systems
- Continuous improvement of work processes and business systems
- Strategic planning and goal setting
- Problem solving
- Education and idea enrichment
- Market performance comparisons and evaluations
- Making changes

Many of the learning companies mentioned in this book (Whirlpool, Rover, National Semiconductor, Caterair, Arthur Andersen) have used benchmarking as one of their most effective tools for acquiring high-quality and highly relevant knowledge.

Internal Collection of Knowledge

The ability to learn from what other parts of the organization are doing can become one of the principal value-added resources for corporations.

Organizations can acquire knowledge internally by:

- Tapping into the knowledge of its staff
- Learning from experience
- Implementing continuous change processes

Two important points to keep in mind relative to knowledge acquisition are (1) the fact that there is not a one-to-one correspondence between what is happening and what is collected. Information, whether it is acquired from an external or an internal source is subjected to perceptual filters (made up of the organization's norms, values, procedures) that influence what information the organization listens to and ultimately accepts. (2) Acquiring knowledge is not always intentional; much is accidental or a by-product of organizational actions. Learning organizations build much more intentionality into the acquiring of knowledge.

Knowledge Creation

Whereas knowledge acquisition is generally adaptive, knowledge creation is generative, the kind of knowledge that Senge says is imperative for learning organizations. Creating new knowledge involves not only group-developed external information, but also tacit and highly subjective individual insights, intuitions, and hunches.

The generation of new knowledge is not the province of only the R&D department; it should be undertaken by every unit and person in the organization. Everyone can be a knowledge creator. Creating new knowledge is as much about ideals as it is about ideas that fuel innovation.

Ikujiro Nonaka, Professor of Management at Hitotsubashi University in Tokyo, writes, in "The Knowledge Creating Company," *Harvard Business Review*, Nov.–Dec. 1991, that "Successful companies are those that consistently create new knowledge, disseminate it widely throughout the organization, and quickly embody it in new technologies and products." He goes on to state that knowledge creation should be at "the epicenter of a company's corporate strategy" (p. 96).

Nonaka has identified four patterns to depict the ways in which *tacit knowledge* (the knowledge we hold inside, but have difficulty in expressing) and *explicit knowledge* (the formal, systematic and easily shared form of knowledge; e.g., product specifications, a scientific formula, a computer program) interact to build or augment the knowledge of an organization.

Let's examine how each of these four patterns produce creative knowledge.

Tacit to Tacit Creation of Knowledge

This is a personalized form of knowledge growth in which one person passes on personal knowledge to another person; for example, a master-apprentice relationship. By working closely together, the apprentice can learn what is known tacitly by the master. This form of learning is a very limited form of knowledge creation. Since the knowledge of the two never becomes explicit, it cannot be easily leveraged by the organization as a whole.

Explicit to Explicit Creation of Knowledge

This knowledge is gained by combining and synthesizing existing explicit knowledge. For example, the company controller gathers and synthesizes company information. This pattern of knowledge creation is a limited form of creating new knowledge because it focuses only on what already exists.

Tacit to Explicit Creation of Knowledge

This knowledge creation happens when someone takes existing knowledge, adds their tacit knowledge, and creates something new that can be shared throughout the organization. For example, the company controller using tacit knowledge comes up with a new system of budget control for the organization. Nonaka notes that the Japanese are especially good at developing this type of knowledge.

Explicit to Tacit Creation of Knowledge

This knowledge creation occurs when new explicit knowledge is internalized within the members of the organization to create new tacit knowledge. For example, the controller's new budgeting process eventually becomes the new way business is done in the company.

In the knowledge-creating company, all four of these patterns exist in a dynamic interaction, a kind of knowledge spiral. These patterns can become very powerful in creating new knowledge since the various interactions can generate much personal commitment and energy.

There are a number of activities which an organization can undertake to create knowledge.

Action Learning. This approach to knowledge creation, as discussed in Chapter 3, involves working on real problems, focusing on the learning acquired, and actually implementing solutions. The learning equation for action learning is: *Learning = Programmed Instruction* (i.e., knowledge in current use)+Questioning (fresh insights into what is not yet known). Action Learning builds upon the experience and knowledge of an individual or group and the skilled, fresh questioning that results in creative, new knowledge.

Systematic Problem Solving. Although most problem solving programs and tools are relatively straight forward and easily communicated, the "necessary mindset," according to David Garvin, Business Professor at Harvard University, is much "more difficult to establish....Employees must become more disciplined in their thinking and more attentive to details." They must continually press for accuracy, and "push beyond obvious symptoms to assess underlying causes, often collecting evidence when conventional wisdom says it is unnecessary" ("Building a Learning Organization," *Harvard Business Review,* July–Aug., 1993, pp. 81–82).

Xerox is an excellent example of a learning company that has mastered this approach for advancing its knowledge base. All employees have been trained in problem-solving techniques and how to use appropriate tools in four areas: (1) generating ideas and collecting information, (2) reaching consensus, (3) analyzing and displaying data, and (4) planning actions.

Experimentation. This form of knowledge creation differs from action learning and systematic problem solving in that it is motivated not by current situations or difficulties, but by opportunity and expanding horizons. Examples of experimentation include the development of original innovations through R&D, pilot projects, and "skunkworks" (independent employee research). Experimentation may be either ongoing programs or one-of-a-kind demonstration projects:

Ongoing programs involve a continuing series of small experiments that are designed to produce incremental gains in knowledge. These forms of knowledge creation are the mainstay of many of the continuous improvement–total quality programs and are usually found on the shop floor. Learning organizations such as Corning and Chaparral Steel have been very successful in creating new technologies through this technique.

Demonstration projects are usually larger and more complex, and generally involve holistic, systemwide changes that are undertaken with the goal of developing new organizational capacities. Garvin notes that demonstration projects share a number of distinctive characteristics:

1. These projects embody systematic principles and approaches which the organization hopes to adopt later on a larger scale.
2. Learning by doing and making midcourse corrections are the norm.

3. They often encounter severe tests of commitment from employees, wondering if the rules and operations have, in fact, changed.

4. They are normally developed by multifunctional, multilevel teams.

5. There are explicit strategies for transferring learning to the rest of the organization.

Learning from Past Experiences.   Learning companies create knowledge by reviewing their successes and failures, assessing them systematically, and transferring and recording these learnings in a way that will be of maximum benefit to the organization.

Research on the development of new products shows that the knowledge gained from failure is often, according to Garvin, "instrumental for organizations in achieving subsequent success....In the simplest terms, failure is the ultimate teacher" (Garvin, p. 89).

Boeing is one learning company that expects its managers to systematically think about the past and learn from both successes and mistakes. The company's 737 and 747 planes had been introduced with serious problems. To ensure that those problems would not be repeated for the soon-to-be-manufactured 757 and 767 planes, Boeing commissioned a high-level employee group, called Project Homework, to examine the development processes of both the 737 and 747 as well as the 707 and 727, two of the company's most successful planes. After working for three years, the group identified hundreds of recommendations that were then transferred to the 757 and 767 start-ups. Guided by the review, Boeing was able to produce the most successful, error-free launches in its history.

While some companies build much of their success on acquiring knowledge from others and improving upon it (through benchmarking and other knowledge-acquisition approaches), others focus almost solely on creating new knowledge. These organizations, such as Rubbermaid, 3M, Wal-Mart, and Merck, find success by being innovators rather than imitators.

Knowledge Storage and Retrieval

In order to store and later be able to retrieve knowledge, an organization must first determine what is important to retain and then how best to retain it. The organization gives meaning to data and information through reflection, research, and experimentation. Knowledge storage involves technical (records, databases, etc.) and human processes (collective and individual memory, consensus). The knowledge stored should be:

- Structured and stored so the system can find and deliver it quickly and correctly
- Divided into categories such as facts, policies, or procedures on a learning-needs basis
- Organized so that it can be delivered in a clear and concise way to the user
- Accurate, timely, and available to those who need it

When structuring knowledge, it is important to consider how the information will be retrieved by different groups of people. Functional and effective knowledge storage systems are categorized around the following elements:

- Learning needs
- Work objective
- User expertise
- Function/use of information
- Location—where and how the information is stored

The retrieval of knowledge may be either controlled (by the memory or records of individuals or groups) or automatic (when situations trigger memories, ways of doing things, etc.). Karl Weick, author of numerous books and articles on organizational psychology and professor at University of Michigan, warns that as a result of the transformational nature of the storage and retrieval process, the normal integration of human memory, the impact of perceptual filters, and the loss of supporting rationales, information that is retrieved from organizational memory may bear little resemblance to what was originally stored. It is therefore very important for an organization to design processes to ensure that the retrieval of information occurs accurately so that a true picture is gained.

As organizations become physically and geographically more spread out as well as more specialized and decentralized, the organization's storage system and memory can become fragmented and corporate benefits of the knowledge can be lost. As work becomes more computer-oriented, the information needs of different organizational specialties become potentially available across functional boundaries. Networked information technology can be utilized so that fragmented information can be reinterpreted and readily exchanged internally.

McKinsey, the highly successful global consulting firm, is a leader in the acquisition and creation of knowledge. They have developed 31 practice information centers (18 competence centers for functional specialties like marketing and organizational performance and 13 centers for industries like banking, insurance, energy, and electronics). There is an emphasis on the systematic development of consultant skills so that McKinsey will have as much internal knowledge on demand as possible. The organization has created the ability to tap systematically into what people have learned. To optimize the capturing of McKinsey knowledge, workers are rewarded for putting their learning into the practice information center databases.

Knowledge Transfer and Utilization

In as much as information is power, the transfer of knowledge is indispensable for the learning organization. Knowledge should be disseminated and diffused appropriately and quickly throughout the organization.

Knowledge transfer and utilization involves the mechanical, electronic, and interpersonal movement of information and knowledge both intentionally and unintentionally.

Intentional Transfer of Knowledge

Intentional ways of transferring knowledge include:

1. Individually written communication (memos, reports, letters, open-access bulletin boards).

2. Training (internal consultants, formal courses, on-the-job training)

3. Internal conferences

4. Briefings

5. Internal publications (video, print, audio)

6. Tours (especially for large, multidivisional organizations with multiple sites that are tailored for different audiences and needs)

7. Job rotation/transfer

8. Mentoring

Unintentional Transfer of Knowledge

There are also a number of ways in which knowledge is unintentionally or inadvertently transferred to different parts of the organization. Much informal learning that takes place is a function of daily often unplanned interactions among people:

1. Job rotation
2. Stories and myths
3. Task forces
4. Informal networks

If in these circumstances intentionality or planning is missing, potential knowledge transfer is lost.

Factors Limiting the Retrieval and Transfer of Knowledge

There are four factors that may limit the transfer of knowledge in an organization and thereby affect the availability, form, accuracy, and meaning of knowledge in the organization: (1) cost, (2) cognitive capacity of receiving unit, (3) message delay due to priorities of sending knowledge, and (4) message modification or distortion of meaning either intentionally or unintentionally.

One learning company which has become a leader in knowledge transfer is Blanchard Training and Development (BTD). Each year the company sponsors an international conference of their international licensees. One of the biggest payoffs from the conference has been the wealth of knowledge exchange and the sharing of techniques on how to help managers in these businesses to be more effective. "It becomes truly a mind-expanding experience," according to Dale Truax, director of international operations.

BTD also sponsors a staff exchange. In the staff exchange, an employee comes from a licensee's organization and works for a six-month period in a job at Blanchard Training and Development. This fosters a better understanding of Blanchard's approaches, products, and personnel. Likewise, BTD places its employees at various internships with licensee's organizations to learn more about that company, its programs and products, and the organizational and local culture.

Other corporate examples of knowledge transfer include Digital Equipment's use of the company's electronic bulletin board system and Eastman Kodak's regular interactive sessions with over 1000 senior staff members to share knowledge about issues such as transfer results and metrics.

Leader in Knowledge Management—National Semiconductor

National Semiconductor, a company that creates technologies for what it terms "moving and shaping information," manufactures products that connect people to electronics and electronic networks. Market segments include business communication, personal computing, automotive, and consumer audio, and products include personal computers, cordless phones, computer security, auto instrumentation, multimedia centers, and microwave ovens. Customers include many of the global 1000—AT&T, Siemens, Intel, Apple, IBM, Boeing, Sony, Toshiba, and Ford, among others.

In 1991 National Semiconductor was in dire straits. Revenues were flat, plant utilization was at two-thirds capacity, and losses were running at over $150 million a year. Although the company was very centralized with a traditional pyramid hierarchy, there were many competing goals. Information was not systematically shared, and the corporate culture was individual-based. National Semiconductor was, in their own words, "a troubled company."

National Semiconductor leadership realized that dramatic change was necessary. A new CEO, Gil Amelio, was hired. Amelio, who has often told his employees that "either you drive change or change drives you," quickly decided that National would do the "driving" and that the key driving force would be to make "continuous improvement a way of life" at National, i.e., transform National Semiconductor into a learning organization.

A vision "portrait" was developed by National's people with images such as "excitement, empowered, global, leader, learning organization, innovation, excellence, and customer delight" depicted on the document. The vision and complementary corporate values laid the foundation for National Semiconductor becoming a learning organization. The seven cornerstone beliefs that emerged were:

1. Maintenance of integrity and fairness with each other, customers, suppliers, and the community

2. Respect for fellow employees, the environment, and one's families

3. Encouragement of the continuous enhancement of one's skills and capabilities

4. Support for innovation and creativity

5. Learning through teamwork

6. Commitment to personal mastery and excellence in all efforts

7. Making continuous improvement a way of life

After less than four years of implementing these values, National Semiconductor has achieved a spectacular financial and human recovery. By 1995, annual revenues had climbed past the $2 billion mark and profits had reached $130 million. Plant capacity had jumped to 85 percent. The organization structure was flatter and leaner, decentralized with more local decision making. People had unified around mission and values. A team-based culture encouraged risks and empowered its people. National had become, again in its own words, "a learning organization...a great company."

In what ways had National become a learning organization? How did the company build its corporatewide learning? Let's look at some of the deliberate and well-designed actions that National Semiconductor took in building a world-class learning company.

Leading Change Seminars

National's leadership realized that to survive change, its people would need be able to anticipate and be comfortable with change. As a learning organization seeking to do business in a new environment, everyone would have to become open to new ideas and new realities. Amelio encouraged staff by quoting George Bernard Shaw's statement that "All progress is initiated by challenging current assumptions." He challenged "all employees to change the way they think about their jobs, this company, and our industry."

To bring about this new mindset, every employee around the world attended the company's highly innovative Leading Change seminar. At these seminars, participants were confronted with the following questions:

- What does National need to change?
- What are we doing to move toward that change?
- How does the change process at National affect my job?
- How does my job contribute to National's success?

Through the Leading Change seminars, National wanted to make sure that people understood the company's vision. Equally important, leadership wanted employees to know that the company needed their ideas, dedication, and commitment to make that vision a reality.

Corporate Action Teams

On the basis of the ideas and issues raised by National employees, eight Corporate Action Teams (CATs) were formed to:

1. *Establish coffee klatches* at National sites around the world to increase communication and dialogue across divisions, levels, and sites. Especially important was the sharing of concerns and ideas between top leadership and employees who rarely saw, much less spoke with each other in the past.

2. *Accelerate the team-building process* by developing and delivering training seminars on "team leader" and "managing in the team environment."

3. *Develop a project and/or expertise database* to capture knowledge and enable employees to tap such resources.

4. *Create employee representative teams* that included such activities as a T.A.S.T.E. team choosing a new food service vendor for the Santa Clara site and a performance appraisal team in Singapore.

5. *Create an office of the ombudsman* to be a central locus for questions, ideas, and concerns.

6. *Modify the reward and review process* to identify ways to reward outstanding team efforts across the company.

7. *Use training and development and career path identification* to encourage more delegation and empowerment at National.

8. *Encourage employees to take managed risks* so that greater progress and more innovations occur. Risk takers, according to this CAT's policy, "are innovators who create imaginative and unusual ideas and solutions. National accepts that risk taking will not always result in a positive outcome. As a company, we believe that clearly focused risk taking is *vital* to our long-term growth and profitability."

Action Learning Teams

Working and learning as teams is seen as a key to increasing productivity and creativity. Team work is encouraged and rewarded at National. Here's one story told in *InterNational News*, the corporate newsletter, about successful teaming at National.

In National's Salt Lake manufacturing plant, operational costs have been reduced by $16 million while productivity increased by 50 percent. Why? Self-managed teams are committed to continuous improvement and nonstop quality. Each week coaches meet for two-and-a-half hours to examine and learn from experiences relative to goal setting, accountability, and how to give feedback that leads to learning and improvement.

Here's another example from the newsletter:

When the management in South Portland saw that delivery performance was holding National back from providing quality service at AT&T, they decided to do something about it. Choosing eight people from different areas throughout the company, they created a Customer Request Improvement Team to deal with delivery performance.

Team members were chosen from sales, marketing, engineering, manufacturing, and planning as well as someone from AT&T. Meeting for a couple of days a month for three months, the team eventually came up with a list of almost 40 ideas which resulted in four key initiatives: (1) analyzing in new ways the delivery misses, (2) increasing frequencies of lead-time updates, (3) creating critical device lists, and (4) developing Pre-Alert reports.

AT&T, in its *Business Review,* concluded that National had indeed "reached the level of world-class support."

Video Compression Technology and Teamwork

National's Embedded Systems Division has invested creativity, time, and research in the development of video technology. Why is video compression such a stunning innovation? Because the interactive video capabilities of the new products such as document sharing on real time would not be possible without video compression. (The available bandwidth of telephones is too narrow to send real-time motion video, and video data takes up too much storage space.) Video compression is a critical innovation for video playback, video conferencing, and video phones.

With this technology, National is able to develop a document or share information with coworkers halfway around the world in real time. The data is entered on a PC and it appears instantly on their screens. The team members receive feedback immediately. Together they can finalize specifications for a new run of chips or create a proposal for a new customer more quickly and conveniently than was ever thought possible.

Employee Responsibility for Learning

National firmly believes in the potency of empowered, informed employees. The company has committed itself to invest in them, and to provide the resources and systems that support and reward them for developing their personal skills. On the other hand, employees must be responsible throughout their careers for acquiring and improving their own competencies so that they can remain valuable to National.

Knowledge Acquisition and Innovation

In order to be able to shape and move technologies, National realizes that it must also shape and move knowledge throughout the company. Ongoing efforts are undertaken to identify best practices and new concepts from all over the world, which are then systematically disseminated throughout the organization.

National clearly realizes that it will not reach its vision by using only existing knowledge and technology. Therefore significant investments are being made in increasing the breadth, depth, and effectiveness of the company's knowledge. Innovation has become a rallying cry for National's success. As CEO Gil Amelio says, "National must be the innovator that brings the greatest value to customers....Innovation can be a new process, a new package, or a service."

National has identified eight keys that it uses to encourage innovation:

1. Emphasize diversity in ideas, skills, and people and makes innovation a top corporate goal.
2. Openly tolerate risks and celebrate failure as a learning opportunity (projects fail, people don't).
3. Promote an innovation process that is clear, funded, and supported.
4. Establish corporate labs where development of patents and other intellectual property is highly valued.
5. Provide project champions who work with small, dedicated, multi-functional teams.
6. Stimulate new ideas and avoid stifling ideas through ridicule or faultfinding.
7. Measure the result of innovation at all levels, and make those measurements important to corporate success.
8. Develop reward systems that provide clear-cut, significant, timely ways for innovators to win: money, position, control.

In April, 1995, National Semiconductor held its first annual International Technology and Innovation Conference for the purpose of encouraging National's technologists to create and share core technologies to further National's *Aspiration 2000* technology roadmap. Papers were presented in the following areas:

Circuit design and simulation

Manufacturing

Device technology and architecture

Process technology

Packaging

Test systems and methodologies

System and software development

Knowledge Storage

Like many organizations, National was overwhelmed with information, retaining data that was not needed and losing valuable data that should have been stored. Staff was uncertain as to what to remember and what to leave behind. In order to cure its "corporate amnesia," the company has begun developing a corporate database and storage system, which was described in a recent issue of *InterNational News:*

> Imagine a city block filled with many different libraries. Stacked on those miles of shelves are millions of books and articles, tons of art and graphics, even videotape, film and audio recordings. Now imagine that you want to seek information, but you have only a single library card, and can enter just one of those libraries. Worse yet, you have heard that other, better libraries exist in other cities around the world, but you have no idea where they are, or what's in them.
> Frustrating, isn't it?
> That was the knowledge storage and access situation at National until recently. Now mountains of information stored at different computer systems can be made available to staff throughout the company via a new project called "Knowledge at the Desktop."
> Employees now have access to all kinds of information such as business plans, materials data, customer support, field sales, public relations and human resources data. They also have access to information from media sources, Sematech, news wires, patent and research records, and bibliographies. Not only text, but graphics, sound, and even video will be available. Fulcrum, a sophisticated new computer program, enables employees to access information on any National system, from whatever type of terminal or workstation is at one's desk. A special corporate action team has successfully worked to "create an easy method for people to find their way through the information jungle," according to Mary Holland, Manager of the National Technical Library.

Knowledge Sharing Rallies

National Semiconductor has created a culture that shares, learns from each other, recognizes, and creates a cycle of continuous learning. One very powerful and vibrant technique (learned from Milliken Company) is to have "sharing rallies" to be held at every National site, with winning ideas moving up to the regional and, eventually, global levels. Sharing rallies are conferences in which employees or teams are encouraged to share their improvement programs, successful and unsuccessful risks, and quality enhancements with fellow employees.

Here's how the 1995 National Pursuit of Excellence Asia Pacific Regional rally sharing was described in *International News*, March/April, 1995, p. 19:

> From the welcoming drum beats and dancers to the emotional closing ceremony, employees shared and, yes, stole ideas shamelessly at the first National Pursuit of Excellence Asia Pacific regional sharing rally, held in Cebu, Philippines, January 8–10....Since July, 1994, sharing rallies have been held at every Asia Pacific site, involving 200 teams and 2,500 employees. In addition to the 12 National Semiconductor presentations, a team from Texas Instruments, Philippines, presented details of their training program for manufacturing specialists.

Some of the presenting teams and the accomplishments shared at this rally are shown in Figure 6-2.

Team	Accomplishment
GMS	Cross-functional team formed to identify areas for improvement with General Motors Singapore
SMILE (Self-Managed in Lean Environment)	Pareto analysis used to eliminate mold flashing at frame edges
1st Team TPM	Reduced manufacturing specialist setup from 10 to 3 steps and setup time from 25 to 3 minutes
SO-8 Power	Various problem-solving techniques and teamwork approaches to resolve operational and business issues
Waste Busters	Formed a cross-functional team to find ways to reduce pollutants, simplify manufacturing processes, and save money
LOTT	Pioneered finished goods distributions from factories direct to customers using logistics expertise

Figure 6-2. Sharing at Asia Pacific rally.

As the team from Malacca, Malaysia, noted, "[We] realize that each of us contributes to the success of our corporation." Other participants made statements such as, "There was so much learning....I'm glad to see the power of National associates making this a great place to work," and "The whole concept of the conference and the sharing and learning that happened was an enlightening experience" (*International News* March–April, 1995, p. 23).

National Semiconductor University

The most recent foundation stone for the construction of National as a learning organization was unveiled in late 1994—National Semiconductor University (NSU). According to its charter, this center-piece for corporate learning is responsible for "worldwide leadership, technical, business, and skills education and training." The University is also chartered with developing a global network of employees who are engaged in learning. It partners with academic and community institutions to codevelop programs and classes. In addition, NSU involves National's customers and the community in the learning process.

The specific goals of National Semiconductor University are to:

- Foster strategic and systematic modes of thought
- Nurture a corporate culture of learning and risk taking
- Support employee ownership of personal career development goals
- Incorporate the best of contemporary information technology in support of lifelong learning
- Be the center of a global learning network
- Promote a shared vision among all employees

NSU leadership realized that employees were going to need a whole new set of skills and competencies to help National become more competitive in a fast-changing global environment. According to Kevin Wheeler, director of NSU, "We needed to find a way to stimulate *quantum* improvement,...doing totally different things, not merely improving the quality with which you do the same things."

To identify the services and resources that would be provided by NSU, Wheeler and his staff (1) identified competencies and skills needed by National from its customers, employees, and suppliers and (2) benchmarked what leading-edge corporate universities such as those at Motorola and GE were doing.

From the beginning the university was seen as much more than just a training center, as just a place for disseminating learning developed by other people. Rather, according to Wheeler, NSU's role is to "generate original, new learning—to do research, to become a generator of new ideas for the corporation that relate to its activities and vision....NSU is a creator and shaper of intellectual capital...which is increasingly becoming the real wealth of a company."

National Semiconductor has built a variety of relationships with academic institutions in the belief that academic institutions and corporate universities have much to offer each other. Corporations can benefit from academic rigor and National Semiconductor would gain a deeper understanding of research and theory in the academic environment. Collaborations have already begun with institutions such as University of Michigan, MIT, Stanford, University of California at Berkeley, George Washington University, and Santa Clara as well as the Singapore Institute of Management and universities in Malaysia.

In related educational alliances, National Semiconductor has done the following:

- Put together partnerships for offering undergraduate and graduate degrees for employees on site. Presently over 300 employees are involved, and more than 50 have graduated since the inception of these programs in 1993.

- Formed an advisory board on which several deans and professors sit to help oversee the quality of the curricula and to bring outside views and opinions to the decision-making process. These advisory board members are among the foremost leaders in industry and institutions of higher learning.

- Created opportunities for joint research and experimentation in educational methodologies. By partnering with National, teachers and professors of local high schools and colleges are offered well-equipped and staffed laboratories in which to try out the latest ideas. National Semiconductor benefits by being the first to learn new techniques.

An important role of NSU is to capture and disseminate knowledge. According to Wheeler, the university also sees a need to "critically examine this knowledge to see what we can learn from it, and then to share with our employees around the world what National has learned. NSU must give people both the knowledge and the courage to run corporate three-minute miles."

As common learning needs are identified, NSU works with its regional sites to codevelop and deliver the appropriate training in a consistent manner throughout the organization. NSU is more than just instruction. It is a proactive system that draws human resource development professionals from every segment of the organization into collaborative, problem-solving teams.

NSU conducts a large and varied number of seminars in areas such as leading change, finance, leadership, career development processes, competency development model, and best practices.

NSU worldwide systems and processes provide continuous input as a framework for future initiatives as well as a mechanism to track and assess its efforts. As a result, NSU's curriculum rides the leading edge of global trends in business and technology, helping to create and sustain National's competitive advantage at a strategic level.

On an ongoing and informal basis, NSU encourages and practices knowledge sharing—whether it be through worldwide events, where people get together (either electronically or physically) to talk about what the company is doing on different issues and themes, or in the various learning rooms of the University. Wheeler has noted that these rooms are more often used for discussions and knowledge sharing than they are used for the more traditional knowledge giving.

Technology at National Semiconductor University

The new $4 million Media Center at National Semiconductor University is a learning technologist's dream facility. Using full-motion video, two-way audio and fiber-optic phone lines, instructors can beam a multitude of media-based images to 12 video conference sites around the globe, from Europe to Southeast Asia to Ireland and throughout the United States. Up to 150 students sit in videoclassrooms, connected to the center via interactive keyboards and microphones to ask questions and provide responses. From the control center, the instructor can ask random questions or zero in on a specific student; change camera shots from personal lecture to items of interest in the studio; alternate between video disc or computer-generated graphics; and instantly gather and disseminate quiz answers generated by students and even provide a visual graph of the responses.

NSU transcends the limits of traditional corporate training and leadership development. It stimulates new ways of learning and sharing. It fosters and teaches a systems approach to business strategy and employee development.

National Semiconductor as a Leading Learning Organization

National Semiconductor knows that the demands of today's global marketplace impose higher standards of business capability than ever before. As a consequence, success on the world stage requires that companies become learning organizations. They must be well prepared for and skilled at driving change, in applying state-of-the-art information technologies and skill-building techniques.

Companies which can generate original thinking from their own activities and the activities of others, which can critically examine their own assumptions, which are aware of the world and the competition and the customer, are truly learning organizations. National Semiconductor has done all that, and has thus become a leader among corporate learners.

Top Ten Strategies for Knowledge Management

1. Create Expectation That Everyone Is Responsible for Collecting and Transferring Knowledge

In learning organizations, everyone should be encouraged to use their antenna to gather data. All employees should become aware of what knowledge might benefit the organization so that they can "rope it in" as it goes by.

This knowledge may be obtained through formal channels like conferences, through the Internet, or in newspapers and journals as well as through informal channels such as social gatherings, museums, and movies.

Some companies encourage and reward research among staff, realizing that in-depth analysis can be leveraged into significant learning power. One learning organization even encourages employees to use part of their vacation time for helping the organization learn. For example, a hospital employee who was vacationing in Singapore was asked to visit hospitals there to learn about some of their personnel policies. Of course, part of the employee's airfare was paid by the hospital.

2. Systematically Capture Relevant Knowledge External to the Organization

Learning organizations avoid the not-invented-here syndrome and systematically seek outside resources in order to gather information that can help the organization. These external ventures may include study missions to better understand the performance and distinctive skills of other organizations, benchmarking of best practices in the industry, and attending conferences and forums.

Whirlpool, which has made benchmarking an important tool for knowledge acquisition, benchmarks companies which are the world's most successful and admired companies, i.e., those in the top 25 percent of performing companies in areas such as total quality, people commitment, innovation and growth, and customer satisfaction.

3. Organize Learning Events within the Organization to Capture and Share Knowledge

Learning organizations have developed many tactics to encourage the sharing of internal learning across the entire organization. For example, as we noted earlier in this chapter, National Semiconductor holds organized sharing rallies in which employees or teams are encouraged to share their best ideas and practices for improving programs, products, and services.

Other strategies to consider are the following:

- Strategic reviews which examine the changing competitive environment and the company's product portfolio, technology, and market position
- Systems audits, which review the health of large, cross-functional processes and delivery systems
- Internal benchmarking reports, which identify and compare best-in-class activities within the organization
- Jamborees or symposiums, which bring together customers, suppliers, outside experts, or internal groups to share ideas and learn from one another

4. Develop Creative and Generative Ways of Thinking and Learning

Albert Einstein wrote that "imagination is more important than information." Increasing a company's knowledge by learning only from others will generally lead to gradual, quantitative improvement. However, generating new thinking and knowledge are where the quantum improvements surface.

Consider some of the following activities to encourage generative and creative learning in your organization:

- Deliberately installing small-scale experiments and feedback loops to increase learning process and achieve continuous improvement
- Rewarding efforts that are imaginative and risky
- Conducting workshops on creativity and use of right-brain thinking
- Encouraging a multitude of ideas to harvest a single good one

5. Encourage and Reward Innovations and Inventions

"Companies will die unless they can create a continuous stream of new products and services," declares Alvin Toffler, author of *Powershift*. To survive in the global marketplace, organizations have to continually create new ways of producing better products and services. Inventions and innovations will be imperative since no existing market share will be safe, no product life will be indefinite.

Yet, too few of our organizations have stressed the critical significance of inventing new knowledge. Kenichi Ohmae of McKinsey laments the fact that people have forgotten how to invent.

Learning organizations emphasize the critical importance of generative learning for organizational learning and success and encourage experimentation and reflection. 3M allows up to 10 percent of an employee's time to invent. Chapparrel Steel encourages experimentation whenever possible. Sony has established a policy that whenever the company introduces a new product, it sets a "sunset" date on which it will deliberately abandon that product. This immediately triggers work on developing replacement offerings. The objective is to create three new products for every one that is phased out: whether it be an incrementally improved old product, a new spinoff product from the original, or an entirely new innovation.

6. Train Staff in Storage and Retrieval of Knowledge

Many of us are still computer illiterate. We barely appreciate, much less understand, the tremendous power that computers possess to code and store knowledge for the organization. Since we are not fully aware of the memory and value system of the organization, we do not know what data to retain or put into a centralized information system. Finally, we may not realize the potency of knowledge and therefore have not taken the time to add knowledge to the organization or seek to discover what knowledge is available either inside or outside the company's computer base.

People in learning organizations are informed as to the critical knowledge needed by the company, its values and memory system, its resources for storing knowledge. They learn how to connect with the knowledge centers and how to access necessary data from all over the world.

7. Encourage Team Mixing and Job Rotation to Maximize Knowledge Transfer across Boundaries

One of the most effective ways to transfer knowledge in an organization is to transfer the individuals or teams possessing the knowledge, whether it be technical, interpersonal, or managerial knowledge. People transfer is powerful because the person carrying the knowledge has the capacity to assure that the knowledge has indeed been transmitted.

Another benefit of team mixing and job rotation is the freshness of approach and perception that the new person brings to the situation. He or she is more likely to raise the "dumb" questions that lead to new insights about how best to handle a problem.

8. Develop a Knowledge Base around the Values and Learning Needs of the Organization

Unless information is coded and stored in a way that makes sense to individuals and the organization, it is only cumbersome data. Too many organizations remain overwhelmed and inundated with vast amounts of data that clutter up the information highway. To determine what data can be used, the organization must decide what is of value and then code the data based on learning needs as well as organizational operations.

The knowledge stored should be easily accessible across functional boundaries. It should be structured and organized so the users can find concise information in a quick fashion. Finally, the knowledge stored should be updated so it remains accurate and valid.

Store the knowledge not only by topical categories, but also according to the learning needs of staff, the organizational goals for continuous improvement, and user expertise.

9. Create Mechanisms for Collecting and Storing Learnings

All too often, valuable learnings, whether from successes or heart-wrenching failures, never leave the minds of the involved individual or group. Learning organizations know how to capture these learnings through a variety of positive and punitive methods. Consider some of the strategies used by global consulting giant McKinsey, which Tom Peters calls one of the best knowledge management companies in the world:

- A director of knowledge management has been appointed to coordinate company efforts in creating and collecting knowledge.
- Knowledge transfer is seen as a professional responsibility and part of everyone's job.
- Knowledge development is included in the personnel evaluation process.
- An employee does not get a billing code until he or she has prepared a two-page summary of how and what the person has learned from the project.
- Every three months, each project manager receives a printout of what he or she has put into the company's Practice Information System.
- An on-line information system called the Practice Development Network (PDNet) is updated weekly and now has over 6000 documents. Documentation also includes the Knowledge Resource Directory (McKinsey's Yellow Pages) that provides a guide to who knows what.
- For any of the 31 practice areas of McKinsey, one will be able to find the list of members, experts, and core documents.
- A McKinsey Center *Bulletin* appears at a rate of two to three times per week for each of the practice areas, featuring new ideas and information that a particular practice area wants to "parade" in front of all the company's staff.

10. Transfer Classroom Learning to the Job

According to Mary Broad and John Newstrom in their classic *Transfer of Training*, less than 10 percent of the learning that occurs in the classroom is ever transferred to the job. This percentage can be significantly increased by implementing a deliberate strategy of learning transference that includes specific steps that the manager, participant, and trainer does before the course (guidelines for what to expect from the course and how to prepare for it), during the course (what skills and tools to practice), and after the course (follow-on activities).

Examples of possible actions include:

Manager

Before—Familiarize yourself with the course and discuss planned use of learnings.

During—Protect learner from work-related interruptions.

After—Develop opportunities for learner to use new behaviors immediately on job.

Learner

Before—Confer with manager and previous trainees on course objectives, content, process, and job application.

During—Maintain an ideas-and-application notebook to note key concepts and applications to the job.

After—Regularly assess your performance and give yourself "strokes" for progress.

Trainer

Before—Confer with supervisors on possible barriers to transfer of training back on the job and identify ways to reduce or eliminate.

During—Help learners form mutual support groups to learn together and help each other back on the job.

After—Contact learners to provide support and help with problems in transferring new skills to the job.

7

Adding Technological Power to Organizational Learning

Alvin Toffler, in his book *Powershift,* notes that the advanced global economy could not run for 30 seconds without the technology of computers and other new and rapidly improving technologies for production. Soon supercomputers capable of one trillion calculations per second will augment even further the capability of organizations to produce and to learn.

Brian Quinn, author of *The Intelligent Organization,* calls technology *the* most important ingredient for managing organizational knowledge. Understanding technologies and using them requires an appreciation of the arts and sciences of learning, discovery, communications, information technology, and computer science.

It will also be crucial for learning organizations to examine research findings and new practices related to neuroscience, adult development, and psychology, as well as advances in computer software and hardware that help people act as teams regardless of geographic and discipline differences.

Organizations that know how to harness technology to enhance their learning capacity will possess a decided competitive advantage.

The technological subsystem of the learning organization includes the supporting, integrated technological networks and information tools that allow access to and exchange of information and learning. It includes technical processes, systems, and structure for collaboration, coaching, coordination, and other knowledge skills. It also includes electronic tools and advanced methods for learning, such as computer conferencing, simulation, or computer-supported collaboration, creating "knowledge freeways."

In this chapter, we will explore three distinct dimensions of technology as they relate to learning organizations: information technology, technology-based learning, and electronic performance support systems (See Figure 7-1).

Information technology is the computer-based technology used to gather, code, process, store, transfer, and apply data between machines, people, and organizations.

Technology-based learning refers to the video, audio, and computer-based multimedia training for the delivery and sharing of knowledge and skills away from the job site.

Electronic Performance Support Systems (EPSS) use databases (text, visual, or audio) and knowledge bases to capture, store, and distribute information throughout the organization so as to help workers reach the highest level of performance in the fastest possible time, with the least personnel support. The system consists of several components including, but not limited to, interactive training, productivity and application software, and expert and feedback systems.

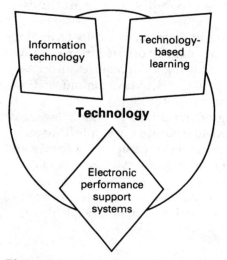

Figure 7-1. Technology subsystem.

Information Technology

Information technology presents new strategic opportunities for organizations to learn on a corporatewide basis. It enables companies to automate (which lessens costs), informate (which provides information that can be used to get a job done, generates new information as a by-product, and develops new information), and transform themselves. Information technology permits the redistribution of power, function, and control to wherever they are most effective. Production, coordination, and management can be accomplished better, easier, and more quickly.

Information technology allows us to break many of the old rules of management, change, development, and learning. Here are the new rules:

- Information can appear simultaneously in as many places as needed.

- A generalist can do the work of an expert.

- Organizations can simultaneously reap the benefits of centralization and decentralization.

- Decision making is part of everyone's job.

- Field personnel can send and receive information wherever they are.

- Plans can be revised instantaneously.

Information Technology and the Flow of Knowledge

Information technology can be a key mechanism for transferring knowledge throughout the organization. First, information technology can improve the ability of people to communicate with one another because it blurs the boundaries of the company and increases the range of possible relationships beyond hierarchies. Second, information technology makes it easier for people to communicate directly with one another across time and space through such media as electronic mail and video conferencing. Third, it reduces the number of management levels needed in the hierarchy, yet at the same time providing an enhanced potential for span of control. Empowered with information, the frontline workers can become much more autonomous. Finally, information technology contributes to flexibility with mobile work stations, relational databases, and the storage of knowledge in open databases rather than in the minds of individuals.

Information technology is a powerful tool for improving organization communication and therefore knowledge flow and learning. A computer-mediated communications systems utilizes the storage, processing, and retrieval capabilities of the organization's information system for internal and external communications. Database, texts, articles, reports, manuals, and directories can be held for quick and easy access by all workers.

Information communications software, including electronic mail, bulletin boards and conferencing, allows for one-to-one interaction and for interactions among dispersed groups. It also provides an electronic learning environment where all members have equal access to data and are able to communicate freely.

If all the organization's personal computers are networked through the mainframe with relevant external systems, any person can take part in gathering and transferring knowledge. Remote access to national and global knowledge networks can be made available within the organization at any time.

Sharing information on a virtual real-time basis and encouraging wider access to information requires the following:

- Creating on-line databases that can be used across functional boundaries
- Hooking into on-line databases and electronic bulletin boards external to the organization, such as universities and other learning centers
- Installing an electronic mail culture and promoting its widespread use
- Using electronic data interchange to create comprehensive electronic network systems

Impact of Information Technology on Organizations

Michael Morton, professor of Management at MIT (Massachusetts Institute of Technology) and editor of *The Corporation of the 1990s,* identifies six major impacts of information technology upon the workplace and workplace learning:

1. Information Technology Changes the Way Work Is Done.

Basic changes result in production, coordination, and management because of information technology.

Production work (how to do it) is affected by physical supports such as robotics, process control instrumentation, and intelligent sensors; by information production such as data processing; and by knowledge resources such as CAD/CAM tools.

In *coordination work* distance and time (time zones) can be shrunk to zero. The organization`00s memory (command database) can be maintained over time, contributed to from all parts of the organization, and made available to a wide variety of authorized users.

Management becomes more flexible. Information technology gives management a better sense of changes in the external environment, and it allows leaders to stay in close touch with the organization's members. Relevant, timely information can be crucial for the organization's direction-setting process.

Information technology also allows more control in two key aspects: (1) *measurement* (measuring the organization's performance along whatever set of critical success factors has been defined as relevant), and (2) *interpretation* (interpreting such measures against the plan and determining what actions to take).

2. Information Technology Enables Integration of Business Functions. Integration of business functions is enabled at every level within the organization and between organizations. This can be done in four forms:

- *Within the value chain.* For example, Xerox connects design, engineering, and manufacturing personnel within its system of local area networks and creates a team focusing on one product. Such teams can finish tasks in a shorter time and with greater creativity and higher morale. With information technology, no part of an organization, in principle, need be excluded from the team concept.
- *End-to-end links of value chains.* These are links between organizations through just-in-time and electronic data interchange.
- *Value chain substitution.* These are substitutions via subcontract or alliance.
- *Electronic markets.* These are the most highly developed forms of electronic integration. The system that travel agents use to electronically reserve seats and to look around for the best prices is an example.

These four forms of electronic integration have, to varying degrees, the net effect of removing buffers. They also leverage organizational and individual expertise.

3. Information Technology Causes Shifts in the Competitive Climate. Information technology adds considerable importance to the functions of scanning and environmental monitoring. Effective scanning of the business environment to understand what is changing in the business environment, is critical for proactive management, especially in an environment that has been made turbulent by rapid technological changes.

4. Information Technology Presents New Strategic Opportunities. New strategic opportunities emerge for organizations to reassess their missions and operations. Technology enables organizations to automate (which lessens the cost of production), to informate (which provides information that can be used to get a job done, generates new information as a by-product, and develops new information), and to transform themselves.

5. Information Technology Demands Basic Changes. Successfully applied, technology calls for changes in management and organization structure. Morton sees information technology as a critical enabler in the re-creation and redefinition of organizations as we know them. Technology permits the redistribution of power, function, and control to wherever they are most effective for the mission, objectives, and culture of the organization. Information technology enables an organization to have all its engineers on the same network. An engineer can share information, ask for help, or work on a project with anyone else in the network. In this way, information technology increases the rate at which information moves and decisions are made.

6. Information Technology Forces Transformation. Information technology forces managers to lead their organizations through a complete transformation process if they hope to prosper in a globally competitive environment.

Shared Computing and Information Technology

Although many companies are still in the shared computing of the 1970s or the personal computing of the 1980s, learning organizations have moved to the networked computing of the 1990s. This new wave of computing by the Net is unstoppable, according to most futurists.

All computers will soon be Web-ready. In theory, this will reengineer all business processes. The Internet will become, more and more, the main arena for meeting, interacting, and conferencing. We will be able to create virtual conference rooms for sharing information.

Technology-Based Learning

Corporate learning in the year 2000 will capitalize on technologies that include computers, multimedia (i.e, audio, animation, and graphics), interactive video, and distance learning (providing one-way video and two-way audio communication between an educator and a learner). The corporate learning environment will be:

- *Modular*, with programs that address a single skill rather than a course addressing multiple skills
- *Multisensory*, stimulating sight, sound, and touch in a variety of innovative ways
- *Portable*, moving easily from home to office
- *Transferable*, moving across languages and cultures
- *Interruptible*, having the ability to stop and start easily

This new technology-based learning will be under the control of the employee. More and more courses will be automated using on-line documentation systems. Employees will be learning more from technology or self-guided learning workbooks than from central human resource development offices. All of these changes will allow employees greater freedom to initiate the types of learning experiences they need to achieve improvements in their jobs.

And why is it so important for employees to have so much more control over their learning programs? Because most jobs within the corporation are becoming ever more complex and require higher levels of skills. In addition, the skill mix and knowledge required will be more and more in a state of flux.

The use of telecommunications in training applications will surely increase. Networked computers facilitate rapid communication around the world, and global learning organizations use extensive electronic mail networks. Electronic classrooms are also available, allowing ongoing communication between trainees and resource persons in distant locations. In sales training programs trainees can role play within a digitally created situation.

Another technology, artificial intelligence, which involves replicating the thought process of the human brain, can observe, guide, and coach users and modify its instructions accordingly. It can adapt to each user's cognitive style, resulting in customized help that corresponds to the needs of each trainee. Training is faster, more interesting, more applicable, and more motivating because it introduces only information needed by the user.

Learning organizations will be employing various technologies to enhance learning. When developing the training environment, it is important to take into account the way learners naturally learn (multiple learning styles; multiple orientations such as visual, aural, kinesthetic; multiple preferences for problem solving). The key, according to Joel Montgomery of Andersen Consulting, is to "allow intuitive entry into the technology systems from multiple perspectives. It is also important to use technology to facilitate learning rather than merely automating a reference system."

Technology-based learning in the classroom will concentrate on the areas to which it can add value—such as interpersonal skills, critical-thinking skills, and generative learning, in which people need to come together to solve problems.

Using virtual reality technology to deliver training modules is especially useful when it allows trainees to view objects from a perspective that would be impractical or impossible in reality. For example, it is not practical or safe to turn a drill press on its side so you see the bottom as a front view. Cyber-training also has application beyond manufacturing or traditional blue-collar tasks; for example, brokerage firms now use virtual reality on the job in real time to train brokers.

The new high-tech learning machines are being called the most powerful learning tool since the invention of the book. The mind is cut off from outside distractions and one's attention becomes focused on the powerful sensory stimulation (light-sound matrix) that bombards the imagination. It becomes possible for ideas and mental images to float in and out of a person's consciousness. While in this highly euphoric mental state, the learning disc opens one's learning centers to peak receptivity while pouring in new knowledge and skills.

With the vast array of learning-based technologies available, selecting the best medium becomes very important. As a general rule of thumb, computer-based training and CD-ROM are generally more effective for knowledge-based skills, whereas interactive technology may be most effective in behavioral training.

A final important advantage of technology-based learning is the dramatic cost savings. Bradon Hall, editor of *Multimedia Training Newsletter* predicts that it will reduce the time required to deliver training by 30 to 60 percent.

Technology-Based Learning at Boeing

At the Boeing Training Center in Seattle, Washington, pilots and ground crew technicians are trained via integrated CD-ROM and laser discs. Training modules are downloaded into the network. Each training carrel includes a Windows-based PC, where laser animation and audio can be overlaid on a computer-generated graphic to stimulate changing scenery or weather conditions outside a cockpit "window." According to Jack Hyde, computer training technologist, this form of technological learning achieves "maximum training flexibility in a constantly changing environment."

Electronic Performance Support Systems

Electronic Performance Support Systems (EPSS) have been called by many the learning tool of the 21st century. It is certainly an essential tool to maximize the power of the learning organization. But many of us are not even familiar with the term, much less with the capability of EPSS in building a learning organization. So let's discover this wonderful new resource for creating corporatewide learning.

Performance support systems can be either manual or electronic, both of which support the worker in learning and improving his or her job performance at the job site. Manual systems incorporate coaches and paper-based texts and tools. Electronic performance support systems use computers to capture, store, and distribute knowledge throughout the organization, helping workers reach the highest level of performance in the fastest possible time, with the least personnel support. The goal of electronic performance support systems, according to EPSS guru Gloria Gery, is to "provide whatever is necessary to generate performance and learning at the point of need."

What exactly does an EPSS look like? It can take on many forms. EPSS can include everything from computer systems that help a line worker in a potato chip factory run and repair any part of the manufacturing process to a customer service work station that anticipates customers' problems and prompts the worker to ask the right questions of the EPSS.

Components of EPSS

According to Scott Levin, author of *Basics of Electronic Performance Support Systems* and noted consultant/expert in the EPSS field, EPSS should have the following nine key components:

1. *Competency profile.* A competency profile is the cumulative record of such things as knowledge, attitudes, skills, and performance levels

for each worker, possibly including the worker's performance appraisals. These profiles serve two functions: (1) to ensure that decisions are made by workers with the right credentials, authorization, or training, and (2) to help an organization's HRD department evaluate employees for new positions, assess performance problems in existing jobs, and know when an employee is ready for additional training or development.

2. *Expert knowledge base.* The expert knowledge base holds both external information, such as industry, market, customer, and competitor data, and internal information, such as employee policy, process, and financial data. Before being stored in the knowledge base, all of this information has to be arranged in formats usable by both the electronic system and the worker. This process is called mapping and structuring the data.

3. *On-line help.* On-line help provides screen-and-field-specific assistance for each program or application in the EPSS. This assistance may be linked to any computer-based training or reference material in the knowledge base. Workers must be able to access this on-line help through a simple and intuitive user interface.

4. *Integrated training and job aids.* All integrated training, performance support modules, or job aids an employee might need to perform a particular procedure are included in EPSS. An explanation as to why a certain decision needs to be made and the analytical steps involved in making that decision would also be part of the program. In this way, EPSS provide both decision-support and problem-solving.

5. *Electronic integrated reference system.* Electronic performance support systems include an electronic integrated reference system that is capable of powerful on-line searches. The system stores an organization's complete documentation including equipment maintenance manuals, detailed procedures, and process guides.

The reference might also include names, phones numbers, and addresses of experts that workers could use for gathering new information or for coaching. Users should be able to rapidly and easily search for any of this material as well as integrate it with any other training or performance support the worker might need before using the referenced information. All of this information should be organized around specific work requirements.

6. *On-line documentation.* As new materials are created or updated, operators can quickly map, structure, and integrate the data into the existing knowledge base. The on-line documentation includes any continuous improvements that the employees themselves devise.

7. *Monitoring, assessment, and feedback system.* This component checks user activity and assesses how appropriate his or her actions were. The worker can know immediately if something is wrong or out of specification, and then can correct the problem immediately. By accessing a worker's competence profile, the system could also indicate how well a particular individual fits a particular job or task and show ways the worker could improve his or her skill level.

8. *Link to external applications.* In EPSS workers can jump easily from one application or software package to another. For example, the system should allow a worker to jump to a word processing program to draft a report, draw in information from an existing database to make a spreadsheet, and then print, transmit, or store the final report.

9. *System information.* Finally, EPSS should be designed with ease of maintainability in mind. They should provide user cues and tools to update the vast amounts of information in the knowledge base, including system changes, enhancements, and new products. Since all new information has to be mapped and structured, the EPSS should have a utility that allows the system administrator or end user to format the data before entering it.The system should also provide information on how the system is being used, what works, what doesn't work, and what upgrades may be needed.

It is important to remember that EPSS cannot work in isolation. There must be available experts (in-company or outside) who can provide advice above and beyond that of the computer. This combination of humans and machines blends creativity with vast information resources. Without this human backup and the organizational learning environment, EPSS will not be able to reach its potential.

Benefits of EPSS for Organizational Learning

There are many ways in which electronic performance support systems can increase organizational learning. Through wise and appropriate application, EPSS can:

1. Help improve the learners' job performance, not just their knowledge.

2. Provide this help just in time, when and where the worker needs it.

3. Furnish instant access to information, methods, tools, and decision aides.

4. Use computer technology to leverage the expertise of a coach or mentor.

5. Accelerate on-the-job training and retention of learning.

6. Significantly reduce training time and cost.

7. Increase flexibility with worker assignments.

8. Enable the organization to train difficult-to-reach workers.

9. Decrease paper documentation, such as user manuals, evaluations, and tests.

10. Increase employee self-sufficiency and empowerment.

EPSS and the Organizational Learning Process

Electronic performance support systems can help build a learning organization's infrastructure to make learning organizations function more effectively. Here are some of the most direct ways EPSS can support learning:

1. *Performance-centered design.* EPSS are designed to enable an individual to reach the required level of performance in the fastest possible time and with the least personnel support. The systems include embedded knowledge, the ability to structure the flow of work, and adaptability to individual performers.

2. *Performance.* The EPSS leverages the worker's inherent intellectual and social skills by presenting information, knowledge, advice, and support at the moment of need.

3. *Individual learning.* As the worker uses the EPSS, he or she can learn in three ways: (1) the worker may change his or her behavior after receiving negative or corrective feedback from the system; (2) the worker may review EPSS modules on the job just before using them; and (3) the worker may review EPSS modules off the job, when mistakes would not be dangerous and costly.

4. *Generation of new knowledge.* The worker will develop new techniques, methods, and procedures on the job that were not part of the original knowledge base. In this way the person creates new knowledge.

5. *Knowledge capture.* As individuals or teams gain new knowledge, the EPSS capture it through some formal process (mail messages, shared databases, interviews with expert workers, etc.).

Technology and Learning in America Today

Information technology is the organization's power tool of the future. This technology, from CD-ROM to CD-I to networked programs and computer-based applications, is to today's economy what the railroad was to nineteenth-century America. Organizations across the world are finding new ways of integrating multimedia to provide learning that is more efficient, less costly, and more flexible than ever thought possible.

New technologies and innovative use of them have enabled learning organizations to quickly leapfrog over competitors. The beauty of marrying interactive technology with learning has resulted in improved retention, increased flexibility, and a greatly enhanced learning.

Corporate Learning Leader in Technology—Federal Express

Federal Express is the world's largest express transportation company, delivering over 2 million items in 186 countries each working day. Headquartered in Memphis, Tennessee, all the numbers at FedEx are large and growing—with over 100,000 employees, FedEx flies into more than 325 airports, maintains 1400 staffed facilities and more than 30,000 drop-off locations. FY 1994 sales approached $8.5 billion. The company prides itself for setting "the standards in the shipping industry for reliability, innovative technology, logistics management, and customer satisfaction." FedEx has received numerous awards, including the Malcolm Baldrige National Quality Award.

Under the guidance of CEO Fred Smith, Federal Express has made a conscious and deliberate effort to build a learning organization. Since 1991, many company staff have worked with Peter Senge at the MIT Center of Organizational Learning. FedEx leaders are quick to point out that in becoming a learning organization, the company has boosted its intellectual capacity, agility, and resourcefulness.

Technology application is one learning organization subsystem in which Federal Express has placed considerable resources and attained significant success. Since its founding, the company has developed and implemented several new technologies to set all aspects of its business apart from its competitors. In addition, Federal Express has made a huge investment in interactive training resources—more than $40 million in 1200 systems in 800 field locations. Each is stocked with 30 interactive videodisc programs, which have been used to train many of FedEx's 23,000 couriers, and 2100 customer service employees.

In recent years Federal Express replaced some of its classroom training programs with a computer-based training system that uses interactive video. This training system can capture and interpret input from learners to determine whether a task is being performed correctly. If a learner makes a mistake, the system recognizes the error, points it out, and shows the proper method.

The interactive video instruction system presents training programs that combine television quality, full-motion video, analog audio, digital audio, text, and graphics using both laser disc and CD-ROM. Learners can interact with the system using a touch screen or keyboard.

The interactive video training closely correlates with job testing. Using the system, employees can study about their job and company policies and procedures, and then can brush up on customer-service issues by reviewing various courses. Currently, there are over 1200 interactive video instruction units placed at more than 700 Federal Express locations. All work stations are linked to the Federal Express mainframe in Memphis. Each location has 21 video discs that make up the customer-contact curriculum. There is virtually no subject or job-related topic that the customer-contact workers cannot find on the interactive video instruction platform.

Once the CD-ROM courseware is written, FedEx knows that it is imperative to keep it updated. The work force relies on the fact that the system provides accurate and current information. For them, out-of-date information is worse than no information at all. For this reason, a new CD-ROM is sent to each location every six weeks. This CD-ROM updates the curriculum through text, PC graphics, and digital audio. Over 1000 updates are made on an annual basis.

Here is a current list of Federal Express interactive laser disc and CD-ROM courseware:

Accepting International Priority Shipments

Agent as a Salesperson

Assisting Customers with Other Departments

Calculating Rates

Computer Resources

DADS and Radio

Dangerous Goods: Acceptance Made Easy

Defensive Driving

Delivering Packages

Domestic Documents

Domestic Services and Packaging

Effective Customer Communication

Fundamentals of Customer Service

International Products and Services

Package Tracking Inquiry System

Personal and Vehicle Safety

Picking Up Packages

Special Services

EPSS Enhances Learning at FedEx

Federal Express customer-service representatives get thousands of telephone calls a day, each of which demands ready answers. In the past, FedEx representatives passed along to another representative customer questions and problems they could not handle. With EPSS, however, representatives can resolve problems "immediately and proactively without passing off any customers" says Bart Dahmer, manager of technology services and technical training at Federal Express in Memphis, Tennessee.

EPSS makes it possible for the customer-service representatives to access one computer application without closing down another. For example, representatives do not have to exit *billing* to get into *customer service*. They are able to retrieve information from several databases and promptly review it on their computer screens so they can address a customer's specific problems.

The system will prompt representatives while they are helping customers. For example, it can enable the FedEx worker to give instructions to the caller on how to measure the box he or she wants delivered, and it can even convert pounds to kilograms, if necessary.

Technology-Based Learning

FedEx recently created a mandatory performance-improvement program for all of the company's employees who deal with customers either face-to-face or over the phone. The primary goals of this program were (1) to completely centralize the development of training content while decentralizing delivery and (2) to audit the employees' ability to retain what was learned.

The pay-for-performance program consists of job knowledge tests that are linked to an interactive video instruction (IVI) training curriculum accessed on work stations in more than 700 locations nation-wide. More than 35,000 Federal Express customer-contact employees around the country are required to take the job knowledge tests annu-ally via computer terminals at their work locations. The tests, which measure employees' knowledge of their specific jobs, correspond with employees' annual evaluations. In fact, the results of the tests make up approximately one-tenth of the employees' performance ratings.

By testing customer-contact employees on product knowledge ser-vices, policies, and various aspects of their jobs, FedEx obtains two major benefits, according to William Wilson, manager of training and testing technology:

1. All employees operate from the same book, ensuring that all cus-tomers will receive accurate and consistent information during each transaction. This helps the company maintain its high service levels and commitment to quality.

2. Managers have an objective way to measure job knowledge for all customer-contact employees.

Federal Express provides many incentives for workers to quickly increase their learning. For example, employees are paid for two hours of test preparation prior to each test, two hours of test time, and two hours of posttest study time.

The current average amount of time that workers use the IVI pro-gram is approximately 132,000 hours per year. This equates to approxi-mately 800 one-day classes with 20 employees per class under tradi-tional training. Yet no trainers are necessary and no travel costs are incurred.

Design of Job Knowledge Tests for Constant Updating

Federal Express also developed a test program called QUEST (Quality Using Electronic Systems Training) to ensure that all of the learning tests are valid, relevant, fair, and meet appropriate learning standards. This was done by creating focus groups composed of trainers, man-agers and job incumbents. The focus groups designed each of the tests, which consisted of multiple-choice questions pertaining to all impor-tant aspects of employees' jobs.

Using the members' collective knowledge, the focus groups created surveys listing the critical tasks for each job. Workers within those jobs were then asked to rate the tasks in order of importance. Focus groups then wrote the test questions based on those issues, being careful to include only questions which directly pertain to activities in which the workers engage.

The final step before implementation of the technology-based learning was to conduct some pilot testing. At this phase, subject matter experts and an on-staff industrial psychologist examined any questions that might be construed as unfair based on the number of workers who missed them. The entire process—from focus-group formation through test validations and implementation took approximately 15 to 18 months.

In order to keep the tests timely, FedEx had the original focus groups meet quarterly to discuss existing test questions to ensure that they were still valid. The groups also spent time writing new questions. Over a period of time, FedEx has built up a bank of several hundred questions for each test. If questions are eliminated, they are pulled from the bank and equally weighted questions are inserted from the same topics.

Federal Express has found that the QUEST automated program saves hours in clerical and administrative activities because the computer does all of the scoring, recordkeeping, item analysis, and score reporting. Additional features of the program are real-time registration, real-time test score reporting, and item analysis.

Success of Interactive Video Instruction at Federal Express

Federal Express, which has invested large amounts of money on technology-based learning, is quick to highlight the many benefits and savings for the company. Internal studies at Federal Express have shown that its system for just-in-time training works. Instruction time on some modules has been reduced by 50 percent with no loss in retention or quality of training. Since the implementation of interactive video training, job knowledge test scores have increased an average of 20 points. Locations that have higher usage of interactive video training have higher job knowledge test scores. When correlating test scores and performance evaluation ratings, Federal Express learned that, in general, the employees who have the highest scores on the test are, in fact, the company's better performers.

Federal Express firmly believes that its philosophy of "train to the job, perform to standards, and test for competency" provides customers with a value-added insurance program that translates into outstanding service and a competitive edge. A well-trained, knowledgeable, and empowered employee supports this philosophy and the company's goal of 100 percent customer satisfaction.

Top Ten Strategies for Technology Application

1. Encourage and Enable All Staff to Connect into the Information Highway

Many people are still ill at ease or unsure of how to utilize the world-wide resources of the Internet. They are not aware of the value and power of commercial on-line services such as Compuserve, America Online, and Prodigy.

But the abundance and availability of information on the information highway is too valuable not to be exploited by all employees. Staff should tap into on-line databases and electronic bulletin boards external to the organizations at universities, vendors, partners, and other learning resources.

The recent emphasis on technology-based learning has inspired an explosion of interactive learning sources. Pepperdine and Penn State universities have established bulletin boards that can network individuals involved in technology-based learning. Professors at Harvard, Clemson, and Chicago are publishing economics papers on-line. In addition, human resource training and development groups abound on the Internet. Many companies offer their training facilities for personal development in off-hours.

2. Develop Multimedia, Technology-Based Learning Centers

Many learning organizations have maximized their formal learning efforts by incorporating computers, multimedia (i.e., audio, animation, and graphics), interactive video, and distance learning (providing one-way video and two-way audio communication between an educator and a learner) into their learning facilities. Technology is also being used to create and support a learning environment that uses the powerful integration of art, color, music, and visuals so that there is a blending of the most effective education theories with state-of-art technologies.

In these learning centers, the availability of computer-assisted learning programs and computer-mediated tutorials will greatly enhance the flexibility for individual learning. Technology-based learning for groups should concentrate on the areas to which it can add value—such as interpersonal skills, critical-thinking skills, and generative learning, in which people need to come together to solve problems.

When developing these new learning environments, it is important to take into account the way learners naturally learn (multiple learning styles; multiple orientations such as visual, aural, kinesthetic; multiple preferences for problem solving).

With the vast array of learning-based technologies available, selecting the best medium becomes very important. As a general rule of thumb, computer-based training and CD-ROM are generally more effective for knowledge-based skills, whereas interactive technology may be most effective in behavioral training.

3. Create or Expand Interactive
Video Instruction

Interactive video instruction (IVI), as we saw used by Federal Express earlier in this chapter, can be of tremendous benefit to learners and the learning organization. Some of the many advantages of IVI are as follows:

1. Training time is compressed from stand-up instruction.

2. Large numbers of employees can now be trained in remote areas.

3. Information is standardized.

4. Travel expenses are reduced.

5. Modeling and simulations can be provided.

6. Employees have access to real-time training.

7. Individualized and prescriptive instruction is available.

8. Competency has been measured by a 90 percent score on all interactive video instruction assessments.

9. Training can be linked directly with the testing system; i.e., a company can see if employees rated satisfactorily on their job knowledge tests by specific topic area of the test as well by employee.

10. On areas rated that are graded low, the employee can receive remedial training and will be provided a list of video discs and manual resources for every category in which he or she scored low.

11. Surveys have shown that employees prefer interactive training to traditional training because it is interesting, fun, requires less time, and is more directed toward the individual learner.

4. Use Technology to Capture Knowledge and Ideas from People Within and Outside the Organization

The use of technology to gather knowledge from people within and outside the organization should be a high priority for organizations. Corning's human resources department, for example, videotapes its interviews with acknowledged experts from within and outside the organization. These videotapes are then made available to staff from all parts of the organization who might benefit from the expert's knowledge, ideas, and inspiration. Corning's Bill Whitmore even created a new name, *tecknowledgy transfer.* for this process designed to identify the technical experts, capture their knowledge, and then transfer that knowledge to strategic places within the organization.

Royal Bank of Canada also uses technology to expedite knowledge transfer through communication channels such as:

- Video conferencing facilities between offices
- The president's forum, a weekly worldwide conference call
- Corporate video network
- Weekly exchange of video cassettes

5. Acquire and Develop Competencies in Groupware and Self-Learning Technology

Improving the quality and decreasing the time of group decision making is extremely valuable for learning organizations. Therefore, it is useful to become familiar with and utilize various groupware software packages that can be employed to manage group processes and group learning in areas such as project planning, team development, and meetings management.

There are also some specific software applications that are designed to promote learning as well as to assist in individual problem solving and decision making.

6. Install Electronic Performance Support Systems

To be developed properly, Electronic Performance Support Systems must be understood by people across the organization. Thus an adequate technological infrastructure should exist, employees need appropriate skills to use it, and development and implementation requires management support.

Be sure that all nine components of a comprehensive and solid EPSS are developed: namely, competency profile; expert knowledge base; on-line help; integrated training and job aids; electronic integrated reference system; on-line documentation; a monitoring, assessment, and feedback system; a link to external applications; and system information.

7. Plan and Develop a Just-in-Time Learning System

As in the just-in-time inventory concept, the theory behind just-in-time learning is to reduce waste and cost and increase productivity by having learning happen as close as possible to the actual time workers need new knowledge. This is especially important because the shelf life of much of the knowledge presently held by employees is becoming ever shorter (e.g., less than a few months for several technical and service areas). Thus the pressure is on learning organizations to develop innovate ways to make learning happen at the employees' moment of need.

To construct a just-in-time learning system, it is necessary to integrate high-technology learning systems, coaching, and actual work on the job into a single, seamless process, and thereby simultaneously reap the learning benefits of centralization and decentralization. These include expert systems (productivity and application software and help, assessment and feedback systems) and decision-support tools. Also electronic job aids and groupware software can add to this self-directed learning system.

8. Build Internal Courseware Technology and Capability

Learning organizations should acquire the technology and capability to design software systems that will support individual and collective learning. These might include self-development systems, open learning catalogues and live resources, career development systems, diagnostic instruments, decision-making aids, opinion surveys, and even means of achieving instant and continuous feedback about the learning of the team, department, or organization. These software systems can then be integrated with other software tools, such as project manager, spreadsheets, databases, and word processor. As such, they become part of the day-to-day activity, language, and know-how of the learning organization.

9. Develop Awareness and Appreciation of Technology as a Powerful Tool for Corporatewide Learning

Many people in organizations, especially older employees, may be afraid of computers and unwilling to regard them as an important resource for their personal and corporate success. They are more comfortable with the Stone Age than with the Age of Technology.

Time and energy should be dedicated to educate these people. Since they may be in senior positions in the organization, they may be unintentionally limiting or slowing the use of technology and thereby the company's ability to store and transfer valuable knowledge. They thus limit the capacity of the firm to learn faster and better.

10. Increase Technological Responsibilities of Management and Human Resources Staff

To maximize the power of technology and thereby enhance the organizational learning capacity of the company, managers and human resource development staff should assume key leadership roles and be knowledgeable about how to:

- Operate technological systems that support organizational learning
- Operate large and continuous organizational change processes
- Be the organization's expert on technology-based learning
- Facilitate outsourcing processes for technological resources
- Facilitate structured on-the-job learning systems

8
Steps in Becoming a Learning Organization

Building a learning organization is a challenge that demands an understanding of and a commitment to mobilizing all five subsystems of the systems learning organization model featured in this book. It is not an easy task, but certainly there is no task more important for assuring the survival and success of your organization.

There is no single, guaranteed way of becoming a learning organization. Each organization must develop a structure and style that is best suited for its own people, history, skill base, technology, mission, and culture. Watkins and Marsick in their book, *Sculpting the Learning Organization*, refer to this process as "sculpting" the organization in the way that best "releases the inner potential of its technology, people, and resources."

It is also important to remember that one never fully *is* a learning organization. Change always continues, and therefore, the need for learning is never finished. What learning organizations do so much differently than nonlearning organizations is practice and perform the disciplines and principles of learning in all five subsystems.

With these caveats in mind, there are, however, some clear guidelines and directions that can be offered to companies seeking to begin this journey. An analysis of the steps taken by companies who have become learning organizations reveals that there are a number of common strategies and sequences of action that enabled them to successfully climb the organizational learning ladder. Intentionality and commitment in becoming a learning organization, not luck or circumstances, made their journey successful.

This chapter presents the 16 steps taken by various organizations in their climb up the ladder of corporatewide learning. Although we will be presenting a list of steps or actions, it is important to remember that they are intended to represent possibilities, not prescriptions. It will be for you to determine exactly what pathway and choices might work best in your organization.

1. Commit to Becoming a Learning Organization

The consensus first step in building a learning organization is for a critical mass of top leadership to become committed to building a learning organization. This group must be convinced that business success is indeed dependent upon learning success. They should remain cognizant of the statement of Harrison Owen that "the prime business of business in today's world is learning, not that making a profit or delivering a service is not important, but than unless learning occurs, they will not be possible" ("Business of Learning," Winter 1991, p. 1).

This commitment toward learning should be based not only on its urgency, but also on the many benefits to organizational and personal success and satisfaction that will accrue. Learning companies are exciting, enjoyable, and fulfilling as well as profitable places in which to work.

2. Connect Learning with Business Operations

The next step is to link clearly and explicitly the process and products of learning to the strategic goals of the organization. Some organizations establish a learning team which advises, counsels, and reviews the overall direction of learning to ensure that it promotes the strategic directions of the organization.

Rover, the large British auto manufacturer, realized that they would not be able to encourage others to get on the learning organization bandwagon until they would be able to define and achieve measurable benefits that would be tied into and would accrue from being a learning organization.

Top leadership in the various other learning organizations researched emphasized how important this step was in the early stages of becoming a learning organization. By showing the direct connections between learning and improved business operations, it was much easier to persuade people throughout the organization of the importance of this new direction. Initial difficulties and challenges would assuredly arise, but the final rewards would more than compensate for those adversities.

Some of the following points should be conveyed to doubters:

- Learning is as much a task of an organization as is the production and delivery of good and services.

- Organizations can learn as they produce; they need not sacrifice speed and quality in order to learn. Production systems can be set up to be learning systems.

- As a learning organization, we will be better able to retain valuable knowledge even if individuals leave.

3. Assess the Organization's Capability on Each Subsystem of the Systems Learning Organization Model

As in most change efforts, a critical early step is to assess the status of the organization so as to identify existing strengths as well as weaknesses, resources as well as gaps. Many organizations have done this informally, but more and more companies realize the importance of undertaking a more comprehensive, systematic examination of their organization's learning competence.

One tool to consider for assessing your company's status is the Learning Organization Profile in the Appendix. This instrument has undergone extensive field testing and has now been successfully used by over 100 organizations from every part of the world.

The profile consists of 10 questions on each of the five subsystems of the systems model discussed in this book. Individuals, teams, or organizations completing the instrument rate their organizations on a Likert scale from 4 (highest) to 1 (lowest) on each question.

For those seeking further information about the use of the Learning Organization Profile, contact Global Learning Associates, 1688 Mooring Drive, Reston, Virginia (fax: 703-437-3725).

4. Communicate the Vision of a Learning Organization

Each of the learning organizations highlighted in this book— Andersen, Caterair, Whirlpool, National Semiconductor, Federal Express, and Rover—developed and implemented a clearly defined strategy to communicate the new learning organization vision to everyone in the organization as well as to stakeholders outside the organization. Everyone had the same "stars to steer by." As many people as possible need to understand, come to support, and get excited about this new vision.

There are several reasons why conveying the vision of being a learning organization is so important:

- The learning organization vision helps establish an overarching goal and purpose for workers.

- The loftiness of the target compels new ways of thinking and acting about learning. It generates powerful, creative learning that leads to high-quality products and services.

- It provides a rudder to keep the learning processes and efforts on course when stresses and frustrations and impatience occur.

- People demonstrate that they can better accomplish things that matter deeply to them.

- The learning organization vision helps to guide strategic thinking and planning for the organization.

Jim Gannon, vice president of human resource planning and development for Royal Bank of Canada, underscored the absolute importance of communicating the vision of corporatewide learning when he stated that "visions are what energize the organization; they are the dreams that pull us forward." The learning vision, like any vision, must be communicated effectively since even "the most sophisticated vision is of no use unless it can be clearly understood by others" (*The Wall Street Journal*, September 12, 1994).

5. Recognize the Importance of Systems Thinking and Action

To build a learning organization, it is essential for people to start thinking and acting in a systems-oriented fashion: that is, to begin to see patterns and leverage points, to focus on how all parts of the organization are interdependent, to see problems and solutions in terms of systematic relationships.

Systems thinking will help organization members see unclear patterns clearer and identify ways to change these patterns more effectively. Systems action will focus on high-leverage changes that may not be obvious to most participants in the system. Unless and until systems thinking and action is endemic, the organization will not be able to optimize the power of corporatewide learning.

The systems learning organization model described in this book is based on a systems approach to change. A company cannot become a learning organization by focusing on just one subsystem or on one part of the organization.

6. Leaders Demonstrate and Model Commitment to Learning

Leaders in a company at the early stages of becoming a learning organization should have but one aim: pursuing improved performance by fostering long-term learning and continuous improvement among the people around them. Learning organizations need the support, modeling, and involvement of their leaders. This backing and, hopefully, championing of organizational learning should be seen as a responsibility, if not an opportunity, for every manager.

Once leadership has become convinced of the value of a learning organization, the leaders must themselves become learning models, anxious to learn and to encourage others to learn continuously as well. The managers should see themselves as coaches, facilitators, and advocates who promote, encourage, and reinforce learning.

In *Sculpting the Learning Organization*, Watkins and Marsick recommend that leaders undertake the following steps in promoting organizational learning and creating a corporate culture for learning:

- Provide opportunities for training and practice in organizational learning.

- Support and encourage staff to overcome the fear and shame associated with making errors, and set norms that legitimize the making of errors made while in search of progress.

- Coach and reward for efforts made, and set norms that reward innovative thinking and experimentation.

7. Transform the Organizational Culture to One of Continuous Learning and Improvement

There are a number of approaches that can be undertaken to transform the organizational culture into one of continuous learning and continuous improvement.

Continuous Improvement

A driving force in all learning organizations is the commitment to continuous improvement so as to delight the customer. This is why organizations which believe in and practice total-quality management are already on the path toward corporatewide learning. Learning organizations thrive in a corporate culture of continuous improvement. Why? Because one question is never far from the minds of everyone in the company: "How can this be done better?"

Quality management requires that a comprehensive learning approach is present and that everyone is learning continually how to do things better. A continuous improvement culture is clearly a learning culture.

Motorola laid its foundation as a learning organization when the company made the commitment to the six-sigma improvement process, a level of quality that allows no more than 3.4 defects per million parts in manufactured goods. Reaching that goal (which Motorola has now exceeded) called for constant attention to improving every action and interaction in the organization. It forced Motorola to find ways to keep getting better—and that required them to be better learners and to be smarter as an organization.

Continuous Learning

In building a learning company, ongoing learning should become a habit, a joy, a natural part of work for everyone. Learning should be occurring as an automatic and integral part of production, marketing, problem solving, finance, customer service, and every other operation of the company.

Pledge to provide numerous opportunities for learning. Make the environment safe and fun for learning. By focusing on continuous learning rather than on one-time training events, you will be essentially forging a new relationship with employees, one that demonstrates a belief in them and their learning.

Learning organizations arrange various events (speakers, coffee klatches, panels, tours, videoconferencing, and monthly programs) to be sure that learning is occurring in every part of the company. All of this continuous learning yields a harvest of reflections, insights, and new ideas for action.

8. Establish Corporatewide Strategies for Learning

Quantum leaps in learning cannot occur without corporatewide strategies and tactics for expanding individual, team, and organizational levels of learning. These are some of the most effective strategies:

- *Encourage experimentation.* Let people try new and different things. Provide time and rewards for innovations. Help people feel comfortable with experimenting and motivated to experiment.

- *Recognize and praise learners.* Organizational heroes should be those who have stretched and experimented, who have tried and failed, who have learned much; not those who never "rocked the boat."

- *Reward learning.* Develop reward systems that compensate learning and learner.

- *Spread the word about new learnings.* Gather staff on a regular basis to exchange information, mingle, holds informal meetings, and share learning experiences. National Semiconductor, for example, holds annual events linked to their quality efforts, where teams of employees present their best projects, experiments, and innovations. Other companies write case studies about their successes and failures, and use these cases in meetings and training programs.

- *Apply the new learnings.* Real leverage and learning comes from applying new learnings in hundreds of different places throughout your organization. Organizations must free and motivate people to use what others within and outside the company have learned. Reward those who can apply other people's insights as well as those who come up with new ideas of their own.

9. Cut Bureaucracy and Streamline the Structure

The bane of any organization seeking to gain the power of learning in the workplace is bureaucracy. Bureaucratic ways of thinking and operating kill the energy and creativity and willingness-to-risk qualities necessary for learning to bloom. Forms and regulations for every possible scenario choke off learning. Tom Peters declares that an absolute priority in establishing a learning organization is the demolishing of bureaucracies.

In the construction of a learning organization, the following recommendations should be considered to achieve streamlining:

- Reengineer, in the sense of eliminating any business process which decreases learning, knowledge flow, or people empowerment.
- Build a project structure rather than functional barriers.
- Decentralize; work horizontally.
- Eliminate hard structures.
- Eliminate vertical and horizontal barriers.
- Introduce fluidity.
- Weld all former functional activities into seamless wholes.

In addition, an organization might consider doing as Royal Bank of Canada does. The bank encourages people to eliminate any bureaucracy which is present by challenging unnecessary forms and silly rules, exposing and eliminating systems and processes that discourage learning, and by rewarding and recognizing only those activities which promote knowledge development and improve quality and service.

10. Empower and Enable Employees

Employees need to be empowered (to possess the necessary freedom, trust, influence, opportunity, recognition, and authority) and enabled (to possess the necessary skills, knowledge, values, and ability) so that they can contribute at their optimal level to the organization.

Judith Vogt and Kenneth Murrell, in their recent book, *Empowerment in Organizations,* contend that empowerment is critical in building a successful learning environment since such action "sparks exceptional learning and performance."

Organizational leadership should allow decision-making power and accountability to reside at the level closest to the action point. They should do whatever is needed to free the worker to serve the customer, including the ability to spend significant sums and cross any functional border.

Learning organizations recognize that empowered and enabled employees are essential for global success. Therefore significant resources of time, money, and people are allocated to increase employees' skills not only for the present job but also for future, unforeseen challenges. Some companies spend over 5 percent of payroll for learning programs. Employees are given all the financial, technical, and other data they need to help them take the initiative and be proactive.

Employees are much more comfortable in carrying out the vision and hopes of the company when they feel that they have a major role to play, as well as the necessary skills. To work productively and creatively, the individual has to have the power to do and learn.

11. Extend Organizational Learning to the Entire Business Chain

For learning organizations to truly tap into all their potential sources for knowledge and ideas, they must expand the learning to all stakeholders, including customers, vendors, suppliers, and the community itself. All these groups have a vested interest in the outcomes of the organization's learnings and therefore can assist in validating such learning areas as needs analysis, learning goals, design of learning packages, and the link between learning and business goals.

Learning organizations should schedule and provide learning activities for these groups in ways that fit the timeframe and learning styles of the stakeholders. Finally, companies can help train customers on how to apply the learnings to their workplaces.

12. Capture Learnings and Release Knowledge

Capture Learnings

In this new world where knowledge is power, individuals at every level and in all kinds of companies will be challenged to develop new knowledge, to take responsibility for their new ideas, and to pursue them as far as they can go. The key challenge of the manager will be to create an environment that allows workers to increase knowledge.

Learning organizations provide an array of opportunities and situations where learnings are captured. They create structures, systems, and time to capture and audit such learning. For example, learning-reflection is done at regular times after meetings and during special weekly learning-reflection sessions. Double-loop and duetero learning are a systematic part of organization life. Everyone in the organization is encouraged to seek information, ideas, and insights from other successful organizations as well as from leading researchers.

Learning audits are conducted to measure whether the structures, time, and other resources are available to create, enhance, and capture learning to the greatest extent possible. Linkage of new learnings to organizational productivity is carefully assessed and better links are forged.

Release Knowledge

Knowledge transfer and utilization needs to capitalize on the mechanical, electronic, and interpersonal movement of information and knowledge. To the extent that knowledge is power, the transfer of knowledge from people to people or from database to people represents the infusion of energy and vigor into the body of the organization. Knowledge should be disseminated and diffused quickly throughout the organization, or it may no longer be knowledge, but only delayed misinformation. Workers should also be encouraged and trained to release their new knowledge, i.e., to be brave enough to try innovative ideas and new approaches in their work.

Learning organizations live on the food and sustenance provided by quality knowledge and communications. Therefore, knowledge should be easily accessible whether in person or through information technology. It should flow up as well as down in the organization. There should be lots of open discussions and conversations throughout the company. Consider adopting lessons-learned meetings similar to those held regularly at the Nuclear Regulatory Commission, during which managers share what events and new ideas emerged on that group's most recent trip.

Alan Webber, noted author and consultant on "knowledge economy," goes so far as to suggest that in the knowledge economy, the most important work is conversation, so much so that at learning firms such as McKinsey, conversation is core of the organization. For it is during conversations that much knowledge is transferred as participants are provided continuous exposure to the experience, ideas, problems, and solutions of others.

13. Acquire and Apply Best of Technology to the Best of Learning

Organizations that lack information technology and/or the capability of utilizing it are at a severe disadvantage in the acquisition, storage, and transfer of knowledge. If knowledge is, as we stated above, the food of the learning organization, then technology is the digestive system which enables the food to get to all parts of the body in an efficient and swift fashion.

Technology also affects the quantity and quality of learning in an organization. Learning centers with multimedia technology can be much more stimulating, exciting, and challenging for individuals and groups. Not only will the calibre of the learning processes be higher, the costs will be much lower.

Finally, companies need to introduce electronic performance support systems (EPSS) into the organization. EPSS enable people to learn when and where they best can. They provide learning resources with which the worker creates the learning response. Since EPSS respond to the employee with explanations, definitions, descriptions, demonstrations, practice activities, assessments, feedback, and other resources as needed, he or she can truly learn while producing and/or serving the customer.

14. Encourage, Expect, and Enhance Learning at Individual, Group, and Organization Levels

No level of learning should be neglected in a learning organization since all three levels—individual, group/team, and organization—complement and invigorate each other.

A key principle, of course, is for the organization to encourage everyone to learn. It should be a part of every employee's job. Rover, for example, clearly states that everyone in the organization has two jobs: (1) his present job and (2) learning how that job can be done better.

Top management should expect all departments and employees to assume greater responsibility for their own learning. Organizations should provide continuous learning packages that encourage everyone to view learning as an everyday experience and actively use every available opportunity for learning and development.

Team learning, the capacity of a group to think and learn together, is vital because teams, like families in a community, are the basic learning units in learning organizations. Team learning should be developed with new job assignments, participation in team projects, developing in-house activities, and group assessment of learning efforts. Robert Waterman sees the movement of people in and out of the various functions and businesses of an organization as a key for developing a learning organization. Calhoun Wick and Lu Stanton Leon, in *The Learning Edge,* believe that the building of learning teams is the means as well as an end for corporatewide learning.

Whenever and however possible, learning should be planned and implemented on a corporatewide basis. Organization-level learning is the level at which systems thinking and learning is most possible. Leveraging of knowledge is greater at this level. The linkages of resources and power of collaboration are most evident when the entire organization is of a single mindset, and when the corporate entity has tapped and focused all of its learning into quantum improvements.

15. Learn More about Learning Organizations

Read the growing literature about learning organizations. The Learning Organization Network of the American Society for Training and Development has compiled a list of over 350 articles and books in the field, a list that is rapidly growing. Attend conferences and workshops on the subject of learning organizations. Invite a corporate leader of a learning organization or one of the leading consultants or researchers in organizational learning theory and practice. Arrange for in-house workshops and discussions on the topic of learning organizations, with a panel of people already working in recognized learning organizations or consultants recognized as leaders on learning organizations. Create or become a part of a consortium of organizations seeking to become learning organizations. Identify successful learning organizations in your industry and others, in your geographic region, and in other parts of the world.

Ernst and Young, as part of its efforts in building a learning organization, has undertaken all these options. Recently, the firm held a two-day seminar entitled "Valuing the Learning Organization: A Symposium to Establish the Concepts, Language, and Metrics for Measuring Human Capital in the Knowledge Era." Panelists and participants included many of the top business leaders and academic authorities in the field of organizational learning; they gathered to discuss common perspectives and create action plans for their respective organizations.

TRW and Arthur Andersen have recently held conferences and workshops on how to build as learning organizations. Rover expends much energy and resources to bring in top theorists and practitioners in the field. In addition, the company was instrumental in forming the European Consortium of Learning Organizations.

16. Continuous Adaptation, Improvement, and Learning

As noted at the beginning of the chapter, a tenet that is very clear to those organizations that have already climbed high on the learning organization ladder is the realization that the ladder has no end. They recognize that they will never reach perfection and will never be finished learning. Learning organizations are, by definition, always learning how to do things better, knowing that knowledge is not finite or static, that change is always changing.

Learning organizations are very aware of what happened to many of the "excellent companies" identified in Peters and Waterman's *In Search of Excellence,* i.e., that most of the companies were failing in terms of profits and customer satisfaction, or in some cases, being eaten up or bought out by the competition. Their fatal flaw? They stopped being excellent; they had stopped learning.

Learning organizations realize that they must always keep learning, always be hungry for new knowledge. They know the vital importance of continually uncovering, analyzing, and adapting the best practices of other organizations as well as those in their own company. These companies use all the resources and stakeholders in their business chain. They learn continuously and consistently.

In Chapter 9 we will look at one company, Rover, that has traveled for as long a time and to as high a level of the learning ladder as any organization. Chapter 10 will then provide strategies and secrets for staying high on that ladder.

9

Rover—
One Organization's
Journey to Success
as a Learning
Organization

Neither the corporate learning process nor the individual one is optional. If the company seeks to survive and prosper, it must learn. If the organization and individual seek to make progress, learning is essential.

SIR GRAHAM DAY, CHAIRMAN, ROVER GROUP
First Rover Conference: "Learning to Win"

We have achieved and will continue to achieve dramatic progress through people who are perpetual learners, people who are skilled in the application of that learning, people who are committed to the application of those skills in the improvement of their company.

JOHN TOWERS, CHIEF EXECUTIVE OFFICER, ROVER
GROUP

Rover's Incredible Turnabout

In the late 1980s, Rover, the largest car manufacturer in Great Britain was in trouble. Losses were exceeding $100 million per year. Quality performance was low and going lower; union-management relations were wretched; leadership was seen as ineffective; future opportunities appeared bleak; and employee morale was sinking.

Today Rover is the darling automobile maker in the world. It cannot produce enough cars to meet the demands of buyers in North America and Asia. International sales have nearly doubled in the past few years. Rover has won nearly every award for quality that exists. The luxury Range Rover is the new "King of the Road." The Rover 600 has powered itself into a worldwide best-seller.

Rover now produces over half a million vehicles a year with annual sales of $8 billion in over 150 markets worldwide. 1994 sales worldwide increased by 16 percent over 1993, at a time of only partial recovery in the world's car markets. In the past five years, Rover has gained in shareholder value, seen huge losses turn into large profits ($56 million in 1994) with average revenue per car sold increasing by 50 percent. Revenue per employee has jumped by an incredible 400 percent!

Not only are the company and its workers more productive, but employee satisfaction is at an all-time high and rising. In the most recent employee survey, over 85 percent of Rover's 34,000 employees, or "associates," stated that they enjoyed their jobs, are well-trained, and are committed to improving team performance. Managers are now seen as supportive partners who are making Rover a better company. And, yes, employees want, more than ever, to learn!

What caused these dramatic changes in productivity and worker satisfaction? Top management and employees are unanimous and quick to attribute the new prosperity to Rover's successful journey toward becoming a learning organization.

Let's therefore look at the road Rover traveled over the past five years.

Rover's Decision to Become a Learning Organization

When Sir Graham Day became Chairman of Rover Group in the late 1980s, he quickly recognized the rapidly changing environment of the automotive world—global competition, new technological advances, inadequately prepared employees, and customer demand for quality.

Aware that "as a minnow among whales, Rover would be swallowed up if it stood still," Day and other senior managers decided that Rover had no choice but to become a learning organization.

Creation of Rover Learning Business

The first step chosen was to create Rover Learning Business (RLB) as a distinct entity within the company itself. At the launch of RLB in May 1990, Sir Graham Day noted, "As a company we desperately need to learn." And on that day, Rover served notice to its employees and to the world that corporatewide learning would become the cornerstone for Rover's survival and return to success.

The role of RLB was (and still is) to provide the processes, the resources, and the motivation for the entire company to learn. Its mandate is to ensure that learning is part of every individual's and unit's job and that the learning process is a mainstream activity with Rover—recognized as it should be, as one of the most significant contributors to the company's prosperity. Through RLB's nurturing and encouraging of companywide learning processes, Rover would benefit from the constantly growing pool of experience and knowledge gained by individuals, teams, and departments. These are the key thrusts of Rover Learning Business:

1. *Associate encouragement and contribution.* To stimulate, encourage, and provide ease of access for all associates to "climb the learning ladder" in order to develop themselves and enhance their contribution to team objectives.

2. *Learning process.* To provide leading-edge learning processes, supported by innovative tools, techniques, and materials for achieving major business changes.

3. *Corporate learning.* To lead and facilitate the design, development, sharing, and deployment of best-practice corporate learning based upon internal and external benchmarking.

4. *Extended enterprise.* To support the business objectives of dealers and suppliers with learning support and collaboration to facilitate world-class activities.

5. *World-class image.* To achieve "world best-in-class learning company" by the end of 1995, RLB must lead in the creation and support of this perception through internal and external communications and public relations.

The inauguration of the RLB marked the beginning of what Rover people now call a true revolution within the company. The company began changing from a slow-moving, slow-learning, lumbering organization into an agile, fast-learning, dynamic "success through people" company. The learning culture quickly began to take root.

Establishing Corporate Vision and Beliefs about Learning at Rover

Rover leadership believed that learning would power the company to world-class levels of performance and enable it to be internationally renowned for extraordinary customer satisfaction. To show its commitment toward becoming a learning organization, Rover sought to establish a total-quality culture built on seven fundamental beliefs about organizational learning:

1. Learning is the most natural human instinct.
2. Creativity, involvement, and contribution are fueled by learning and development.
3. Everyone has two jobs—the present job and improving that job.
4. People own what they have created.
5. People need to be valued.
6. Creativity and ingenuity are widely distributed and grossly underused.
7. Management does not have all the answers.

Rover also developed several definitions for determining what being a learning organization would mean for Rover:

> A place where inventing new knowledge is not a specialized activity...it is a way of behaving, indeed a way of being, in which everyone is a knowledge worker.
> A company in which learning and working are synonymous; it is peopled by colleagues and companions rather than bosses, subordinates and workers; and both the inside and outside of the company are being continuously searched and examined for newness.
> A company that monitors and reflects upon the assumptions by which it operates. It is in touch with itself and its environment and thereby adapts and changes as a matter of course, rather than traumatically, as in a crisis.

Aligning Corporate Objectives with Corporate Learning Process

Following the establishment of the learning organization as a part of the Company's new vision, Rover realized that it had to develop clear business targets and benefits that would be achieved as a result of this new learning focus. Initially, Rover identified 20 internal and external targets for critical success, including:

Internal Targets
- $2 million in cost savings through better learning
- 10 percent shift in attitudes in the employee survey held every two years
- Abundant materials and programs to guide the company's learning process
- 1000 employees with their own self-development programs
- 2000 employees ambitious enough to apply for jobs that they think they could do by attending career *walk-ins* (these are gatherings where groups of managers are available on certain evenings to discuss vacancies)
- 500 managers acting as qualified coaches (as opposed to cops)
- 10,000 employees with external learning credits for learning that occurred internally

External Targets
- To be featured in media as a learning organization
- Receive national training awards

Rover then scrutinized each of its key business objectives to determine how corporate learning could become a primary driver in helping the company achieve these objectives.

Aligning Corporate Learning to Total-Quality Efforts of Rover

Rover realized that quality products, processes, and services were vital to its short-term and long-term success. The principles of corporate learning were clearly aligned with the principles of total-quality improvement. Every learning process was to be tested against the following principles:

Continuous improvement. To achieve ever more demanding objectives, there must be a creative application of the learning process and in a shorter timeframe.

Management led. Management will plan for learning and development opportunities for employees in their own area.

Everyone responsible for quality. Involve employees in the design and delivery of learning and development programs by integrating the best mentoring, shared experience, and self-development.

Companywide. Each plant is to plan, invest, and report on its learning and development so that corporatewide progress can be formulated.

Cost of quality. Financial and nonfinancial benefits to the organization accruing from the learning programs would be evaluated and reported.

Leaders Demonstrate Commitment to Corporatewide Learning

Rover's leaders realized that it was important for them to demonstrate their commitment to the concept of a learning organization both through role modeling and clear support. The first action illustrating this commitment was for each member of the Rover Group board of directors to also serve and actively participate as a member of the board of governors of Rover Learning Business.

The board and top managers have indeed undertaken a number of learning leadership roles, such as:

- Sponsoring corporate learning events
- Promoting line managers who demonstrate a commitment to learning
- Funding all employees who want to learn something outside their normal job responsibilities
- Leading learning processes and programs from the front of the classroom, thereby acting as role model
- Championing leadership learning programs
- Giving recognition for learning achievements at all levels as part of the motivation process

Streamlined into a Learning Structure

The old management hierarchy was soon transformed into a structure that featured a lean organization where greater responsibility and accountability were given to individual workers. Greater emphasis was placed on teamwork so that learning barriers would be removed and an environment where there were better working relationships and mutual trust would be created. Each individual was expected to develop and demonstrate a broader range of knowledge, skills, and leadership.

Simplified Policies and Procedures

"If you are a learning organization, the last thing you want is a lot of heavy documentation!" proclaims RLB's Barrie Oxtoby. Rover, like most companies, used to have policy manuals for everything, but no one read them except the people who wrote them. As part of Rover's learning initiatives, the company instead has concentrated on sets of principles, vision statements, and goals. "Change happens so rapidly that any documentation will be out of date before it is finished," Oxtoby acknowledges.

A Corporate Learning Model for Enhancing Business Results

Rover has developed a corporate learning process model that has been widely used throughout the organization. This model is illustrated in Figure 9-1. The 13 steps in this model are described here.

1. Business Opportunity. All learning undertaken should contribute directly to bottom-line performance. Without this there is no justification for doing it. Business opportunities can emerge from two main areas: (1) changes that require considerable financial investment and affect a wide range of people and (2) continuation of existing practices where performance requires significant improvement.

2. Champion. This is the person who identifies with the project's goals, opens doors, motivates, sets standards, maintains and coordinates the key players and expert group. The champion for a major strategic issue will normally be a Rover board director.

3. Key Players and Expert Group. These include the subject experts, experienced operators, motivators, networkers, learning experts, and outside experts.

4. Develop Specification.   This includes business opportunity, aims, objectives, learning process and methods, venues, timing, and methods for measuring for success.

5. Design Process and Plan.   All the major steps which will absorb time, the leader of each step, any milestones, and the resource for delivering the end objective are listed.

6. Prepare Coaches and Learners.   Describe the project to pertinent employees and subject specialists so they are prepared and motivated to carry out corporate learning process.

7. Create the Learning Material.   Develop high-quality materials produced to agreed timing that contribute to complete success of project; can range from a new model to audiotapes, videos, handouts, etc.

8. Prepare Learning Environment.   The learning should be as close to the workplace as possible, but in any case, a high-quality learning environment should be prepared.

9. Implement Learning.   A combination of activities of learners and coaches to capture learning both off and on the job.

10. Measurement.   Measuring the effect of the learning and change process against the original objectives. The bottom-line benefits achieved by a well-specified process will strengthen the value of systematic learning to the organization.

11. Record Experience.   The learning is recorded in a computer system for the organization and in the individual's personal development files.

12. Develop Learning Material.   Develop any learning lessons for future organizational use.

13. New Best Practice.   Revise the best practice standard to share this new experience throughout the organization.

Throughout the corporate learning process, the key players or learners can draw on already established best practice and benchmarking, and engage the involvement of company employees. These are the three bulleted items in the central box in Figure 9-1; They form the foundation for Rover's targeted efforts on building corporate knowledge, which is called the *group learning exchange network* (GLEN).

Launched in 1993, GLEN is the definitive corporate database (updated quarterly by inputs from people in all Rover Group areas) accessible via IBM-compatible PC discs or directly on company computer networks. It guides inquirers to the appropriate sources of best practice or benchmarking information within the company. Also included on GLEN is a summary of personal learning materials for Rover associates.

Communication of Organizational Learning Activities and Programs

To maintain the momentum of building the learning organization as well as to transfer new creative ideas about learning, Rover developed an internal communications strategy that involved a variety of communications:

■ Learning products that focus upon satisfying individual needs to become more effective learners are launched regularly.

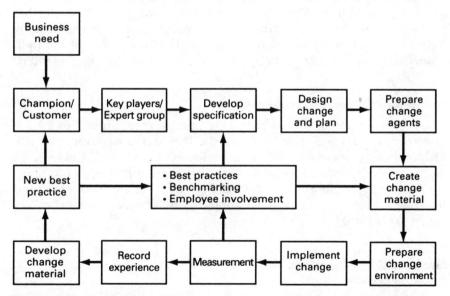

Figure 9-1. Rover Group LTD Corporate Learning Process Model (*Copyright © 1993 Rover Learning Business. Used with permission. All rights reserved.*)

- At least one page of every company newsletter is devoted to RLB and learning activities of employees.

- Every main plant has news bulletins which, without exception, have group and individual learning as a main feature.

- The electronic notice bulletin board at each main plant location features existing and new programs available at employee development centers.

- Company roadshows feature learning as a key employee activity.

- Existing best practices are role-modeled by groups or individuals through presentations and exhibitions.

Empowering People with a "Success through People" Philosophy

Underlying Rover's success in becoming a learning organization is a philosophy of "success through people." In the company's new environment of continuous learning, people needed to be empowered to contribute more to organizational success. Therefore, they needed to receive much more in return: namely, an interesting and satisfying job, improved knowledge through learning and involvement, being listened to, being able to make a greater contribution, having a ladder to further learning, higher self-esteem and confidence, rewards for using learning to improve quality, profits, and operations. Learning needs of the individual associate and the learning process of the company were balanced.

Job Security for Rover Associates

Rover quickly demonstrated that its long-term commitment to associates who learned was more than words. The company introduced single-status employees and job security for everyone. Artificial ceilings and job descriptions were removed. The two-job principle (i.e., performing present job and improving that job) was implemented, and last, but not least, an environment of individual learning opportunities for all was created.

Input and Involvement from Everyone

Rover repeatedly stressed that its most important asset was its work force. A recently opened Rover production facility provides an example of how the principles of openness, empowerment, improvement, and personal development have become embedded in Rover's way of operating:

- Team leaders were involved from the layout of the machinery to the color of the plant's walls.
- Associates are responsible for maintaining work and rest areas.
- Associates are encouraged to get involved with process improvement (to get an idea of how involved they are: each associate averages three suggestions per year!).

Associate involvement is a way of life in Rover as demonstrated by the abundance of quality action teams (QATs). The success of these teams is attested by the number of closed QATs, i.e., those that have completed their task by solving the original problem. Rover estimates these motivated associates saved Rover over $3 million per year.

New Role for Managers

Five years ago, managers pushed for improvements that would meet set standards (which, in effect, became the ceilings for upper levels of performance). This resulted in a diluted execution of ideas and insufficient upward flow of ideas. Today managers serve primarily as facilitators, coaches, mentors, and motivators empowering the real experts, who are the associates. Managers and employees all work together as a potent force for continuous improvement in both quality and productivity. Since 90 percent of learning takes place on the job, managers have significantly increased the cost effectiveness of training through their new capabilities and commitment to facilitating learning on the job.

Managers are encouraged both to build on existing good practice and actively transfer their own experience to other colleagues. This philosophy and practice is called *copy plus*. Total-quality leadership within Rover means that line managers take full responsibility for creating a learning environment in their area, and for coaching employees in all aspects of their learning.

Extending the Learning Enterprise to Customers, Dealers, and Suppliers

Rover realized that intensified industrial competition throughout the world was putting an increasing premium on a company's ability to not merely satisfy suppliers and customers but to delight them. This was particularly true in the fiercely competitive international motor industry.

The company decided not only to learn about their suppliers, dealers, and customers, but to have them learn together with Rover. Accordingly, the company offers courses at various Rover facilities, as well as at colleges and hotels, in an effort to help suppliers meet the auto industry's demanding standards of quality and efficiency.

Significant resources are devoted to learning programs for Rover dealers. These include a library of sales and after-sales skill-improvement videos as well as industry-leading literature and video packages covering sales, product knowledge, and servicing techniques. In addition, service correspondence courses have attracted over 500 participants per year. Rover also offers tutored courses at its various facilities for dealer staff.

Recently, a Rover professional program was launched in quality management and customer-service initiatives. The program provides a structured career path, via a learning and competence accreditation ladder. In its first year, over 2000 dealer staff from over 500 dealerships enrolled in what has been described as a remarkable confirmation of the continuous learning ethos at Rover.

Personal Learning

At Rover every employee is responsible for his or her learning as well as for long-term employability within Rover. This was a successful and crucial mental paradigm shift for the people of Rover.

Training and learning used to be seen by associates as "something that you had done to yourself," almost as if you had done something wrong. It was not seen as an opportunity for self-development, long-range employability, part of continuous improvement related to personal and organizational success. Or to put it in Rover's terms, learning was not seen "as a way of putting the future is in your hands."

Rover now seeks to encourage maximum personal responsibility and accountability in both learning and operational areas. The concept of associate ownership of personal development and learning has been intensively promoted. It was and remains Rover's firm belief that people who are given a genuine responsibility for their own development will in turn build a deeper commitment to the company.

A foundation stone of this ownership concept is the personal development file. Each associate summarizes in this file the learning and skills he or she has gained through experience and formal education.

This provides a solid platform for the personal development plan, created jointly by the individual and manager to meet the career aspirations of the individual and the business needs of the company.

Another RLB initiative to encourage a climate of continuous learning is the Rover employee assisted learning (REAL) program which offers each associate $175 in tuition fees every year for lateral personal development in business areas not specifically related to current job skills. The annual participation in REAL has ranged between 2000 and 4500 applications.

Principles for Learning Application

In their learning activities Rover associates seek to accomplish three goals: (1) enhance job skills, (2) acquire knowledge of new technologies, and (3) expand both personal and corporate vision, thus creating the environment as well as the opportunities for innovation.

Training and career development activities are expected to be consistent with the following principles of learning:

1. *Active participation.* Learners should be involved in the design of their own training and its future application. Prebriefing of learners is essential.

2. *Knowledge of results.* Learners should know how they are doing during and after training. Feedback mechanisms must be in place to ensure that this happens.

3. *Learning transfer.* Where learning is off the job, opportunities need to be created to transfer the learning to job application.

4. *Reinforcement of appropriate behavior.* Learners who demonstrate changes in behaviors should be actively recognized and given feedback as well as encouragement.

5. *Motivation of learners.* Individuals must recognize the need to learn something; and managers need to utilize the learner's own drive and purposes.

6. *Willingness to change.* Visible support from the manager is most likely to encourage the learner to change.

7. *Practice and repetition.* It is necessary to provide opportunities to practice on real-work situations without fear of failure.

8. *Time for reflection.* All learners need time and space to assimilate learning by talking to others and having questions answered— thinking and planning are real work.

Wealth of Learning
Opportunities at Rover

Rover recognized that being the best requires continuous improvement and therefore continuous and multiple opportunities for learning. There would need to be a wide array of choices that would make learning attractive and easily accessible. Accordingly, the company established employee development centers at all eight Rover sites. Each site was fully fitted with open-learning equipment in the form of text, audio, video, interactive video, and computer-based training. The open-learning resources in each center were dovetailed with line-management needs through the personal development review process. The efficiency in responding to learning needs was ensured by the continuous networking of the personal development reviews with the centers.

Today there are over 200 learning programs available at the centers, ranging from basic mathematics to computing, from electronics to languages, from management skills to interpersonal skills, from health-care issues to pension issues. All Rover associates are able to utilize any of these resources during working hours on a directly work-related topic, or after working hours for other areas.

The centers have proven to be very popular—more than 50,000 hours of active learning each year and growing. And the use is not restricted just to those who work directly for the company. Rover dealers and key suppliers are actively encouraged to participate in these open-learning programs, as well as other learning opportunities offered by Rover.

In addition to courses within Rover facilities, a whole range of learning programs for people inside and outside Rover are promoted, such as MBA courses, health and safety training, and overhead crane theory. Several high-quality degree and non-degree programs have been developed in collaboration with the University of Warwick.

In the past five years, over 1000 employees have obtained postgraduate awards from universities. Over 221,000 have been involved in the personal development plan; 12,000 employees have taken advantage of the REAL program, while another 7000 have self-learned with audiotapes.

Materials and Products to
Help People Learn

Rover has developed a number of learning resources to encourage and assist the individual and corporate learning processes. Three especially effective learning tools are the *Learning is an Essential Way of Life* pamphlet, the annual *Learning Diary,* and the *Personal Learning Pays* audiotape.

***Learning is an Essential Way of Life* Pamphlet.** This pamphlet graphically asks and answers two basic questions for the associates of Rover:

1. Why should I Learn? *Answer:* For me it would help: improve flexible skills, my job opportunities, my career, my family to learn, improve my way of life, gain accreditation, my security, in my retirement.

    For Rover it would help with: improved profitability, associate involvement, teamwork, continuous improvement, a flexible work force, improved processes, a lean operation, ensuring success.

2. How can I learn? *Answer:*
    - Talk to your manager about a professional development file—a tool for defining and planning your personal development.
    - Learn on the job, through job rotation, through team work, in small work groups, quality-action teams, and continuous-improvement groups.
    - Acquire manual and trade skills at local Rover training departments.
    - Attend local colleges or training.
    - Learn by distance learning through open university and correspondence courses.
    - Receive coaching and mentoring from managers.
    - Liaise with local school and community groups.
    - Self-teach at Rover's education development centers using computer-based training books.

Learning Diary. Each year Rover associates receive a pocket *Learning Diary,* which in addition to providing space for scheduling one's activities on a week-by-week basis, is chock-full of organizational and individual learning ideas and suggestions. The themes and format for each year's diary are derived directly from associates' suggestions and experiences. The 1995 diary included:

- Power tools for learning
- Managing your learning
- Learning planning and review tools
- Ways of controlling stress

- Numerous learning axioms (such as, "When you can teach someone else what you have learned, you really know you know," and "If you do not live in the future today, you will live in the past tomorrow.")
- Hundreds of practical ways of improving your learning skills
- Resources for learning
- Opportunities and rewards for increasing Rover's learning capacity

Learning Book and Tape.   Recognizing that individuals may have different learning patterns, Rover has made available a *Personal Learning Pays* book and cassette package which helps users to identify the learning style (be it reading, watching, or hands-on) best suited to them. Over 6000 associates took advantage of this package in the first year.

A Preeminent Learning Organization

Rover has grown and benefited immensely over the past five years as an emerging learning organization. There has been a continuous flow of improvements initiated and generated through learning by empowered employees. Learning has indeed resulted in a better bottom line, happier employees, and a superior globalwide reputation.

Although Rover has pioneered many new approaches to build corporatewide learning, the company continues a vigorous search for more ways to meet its aspiration of becoming a preeminent learning organization and accelerating the pace of success through global learning.

Key corporate learning activities planned for the future include:

- Further development of the Rover way of corporate learning, including GLEN and Networks
- Ongoing research and benchmarking of top learning initiatives from around the world
- Creation of a "Change Agent's Toolkit" for use by line managers
- Continued response to the evolving learning needs of associates whose hunger for learning continues to grow

Rover has certainly gone a long way on its journey to become a learning organization. Their global reputation as one of the world's best is well deserved.

10

Building, Maintaining, and Sustaining the Learning Organization

The toughest thing about being a success is keeping on being a success.

IRVING BERLIN

Taking the specific steps to build a learning organization as described in Chapter 8 and demonstrated by Rover in Chapter 9 requires a well-orchestrated commitment and plan on the part of many people in the organization. Maintaining this new, higher level of learning power is, perhaps, an equally demanding challenge, one that requires a serious determination not to lose the precious goal that has been achieved. (Witness how most of the "excellent companies" in the Peters and Waterman study, *In Search of Excellence*, dropped from their high ratings or disappeared altogether because they did not know how to maintain or sustain excellence.)

In this chapter, we will examine four significant questions:

- Where within the organization do we begin the effort?
- How do we successfully continue the transformation?
- What are the facilitating factors that encourage the building of a learning organization?
- How do we maintain the new learning organization?

Where to Begin Building a Learning Organization

Where should one begin transforming one's company into a learning organization? Is there a starting point?

In general, it is preferable to begin at the very top—to get top leadership committed to becoming a learning organization. However, this is not always possible, particularly at the early stages. Some leaders need to be shown first that it works, even if this has to be done at a unit level.

But, if organizations are in fact, organisms, then each small part—every department or site—has some capacity to affect the whole of the organization. Any entry point has the potential to build pockets of experimentation that can get people to work together on real problems that will release their energies, tackle flaws in the system, and help them learn as an entity.

It is possible to begin in any part that has the potential to affect the others. Therefore, start where the energy is! Consider any or all the following actions:

- Work with the board of directors.
- Work out of the human resources department (since they may be knowledgeable and supportive of the learning organization concept and values).
- Establish a joint union-management initiative.
- Set up a series of task forces.
- Run a consciousness-raising development program.
- Work with the strategic planning cycle.
- Begin with a diagnosis (using the Learning Organization Profile in the Appendix).

- Start with a company conference.
- Focus on one of the key business issues.
- Start with one department.

The degree of difficulty in getting the organization to change often depends on one's position in the organization. If you feel that you are not in a powerful position, and that you are working in the middle and at the margins, work through committees and through other structures designed to provide an avenue for indirect influence over decision makers.

It is important for you to answer the following questions:

1. What stage of organizational learning is your organization occupying?
2. What is your position in the organization?
3. What avenues and resources might you use in transforming your company into a global learning organization?

Whatever you do, don't wait around and hope that something magical happens on its own. Take the initiative to start climbing the ladder.

Keys to a Successful Transformation into a Learning Organization

Causing a significant organization transformation is never easy or quick; it is often very difficult. Many organizations fail and drift back to where they were before. The following eight steps to a successful tranformation are crucial. Mistakes at any point can have a devastating impact that may slow momentum or even cause the climb toward becoming a learning organization to be aborted.

1. Establish a Strong Sense of Urgency about Becoming a Learning Organization

Most successful change efforts begin when individuals or groups within the organization look seriously at the company's competitive situation, market position, technological trends, and/or financial performance and realize that a great crisis or opportunity looms. A sense of urgency is essential since getting a transformation program started requires the aggressive cooperation of many individuals.

Over 50 percent of companies never get their transformation effort off the ground because they fail at this first phase. What are some of the reasons for this failure?

- Executives underestimate how hard it can be to drive people out of their comfort zones.
- Leaders lack patience to handle the preliminaries.
- They become paralyzed by the downside possibilities; e.g., senior employees will become defensive, morale will drop, events will spin out of control, short-term business results will be jeopardized, etc.
- Managers are afraid to take the risks involved in creating a new system of operations.

A key strategy at this point is to make the status quo seem more dangerous than the unknown. Until the urgency rate is pumped high enough, the transformation process cannot succeed.

2. Form a Powerful Coalition Pushing for the Learning Organization

Although the aspiration of becoming a learning organization may begin with just one or two people, successful transformation requires a mass of individuals truly committed to this goal.

John Kotter, a Harvard professor who has had extensive experience in assisting organizations in major change efforts, notes that "in successful transformations, the chairman or president or division general manager, plus another 5 or 15 or 50 people, come together and develop a shared commitment....In my experience, this group never includes all the company's most senior executives because some people just won't buy in, at least not at first. But in most successful cases, the coalition is always pretty powerful—in terms of titles, information, expertise, reputations and relationships (p. 62)."

Senior managers always form the core of the group, but oftentimes the guiding coalition for becoming a learning organization may be a board member, a representative from a key customer, or even a powerful union leader.

The high sense of urgency helps to put a guiding coalition together. But someone needs to get these people together, help them develop a shared sense of urgency about learning as an organization, and create a minimum level of trust and communication. Off-site retreats are especially valuable at this stage.

Organizations that fail in this key area have usually either underestimated the difficulties of producing change and the critical importance of a powerful guiding coalition or not developed the ability to work in teams. A learning organization effort that does not have a powerful enough guiding coalition may make some apparent progress for a while, but other important issues soon emerge and derail the change process.

3. Create the Vision of the Learning Organization

A successful transformation to learning organization status requires a vision of the future that is relatively clear to communicate and appeals to employees and other stakeholders. Without this vision, the transformation effort can easily dissolve into a list of confusing and incompatible projects that can take the organization in the wrong direction or nowhere at all.

Kotter cites a useful rule of thumb: "If you can't communicate the vision to someone in five minutes or less and get a reaction that signifies both understanding and interest, you are not yet done with this phase of the transformation process (p. 63)."

4. Communicate and Practice the Vision

Transformation into a learning organization is impossible unless large numbers of the organization have their hearts and minds committed to the challenge. Executives who communicate well incorporate the vision into their hour-by-hour activities. For example, in routine discussions about a business problem, they talk about how proposed solutions will fit or not fit into this new vision; in a regular performance appraisal, they talk about how the employee's behavior helps or undermines the vision; in routine meetings with employees, they tie their answers back to renewal goals.

Corporate leaders use every existing communication channel to broadcast the vision. Previously boring and unread company newsletters are turned into lively articles about the vision (see National Semiconductor and Rover stories in Chapters 6 and 9). They take ritualistic and tedious quarterly management meetings and turn them into exciting discussions of the transformation into a learning organization. They replace old management courses with courses that focus on the new vision. And, most importantly, they "walk the talk" of a learner—

they consciously attempt to become a living symbol of the new corporate culture.

5. Remove Obstacles That Prevent Others from Acting on the New Vision of a Learning Organization

The previous four steps are often insufficient by themselves. Change also requires the removal of obstacles so that growing numbers of people can participate in the change process. There are six major obstacles that are the main culprits in hindering organizational learning:

- *Bureaucracy*, where policies, regulations, forms, and busywork become more important than change
- *Competitiveness*, which emphasizes individuals rather than teamwork and collaboration
- *Control*, which may provide a "high" for those in control, but is always a "low" for organizational learning
- *Poor communications*, which result from filters, conscious and unconscious biases, narrow listening, and delays
- *Poor leaders*, who neither preach nor practice learning, and are most concerned about protecting their turf
- *Rigid hierarchy*, which forces people and ideas to go up and down narrow silos

In the early stages of becoming a learning organization, few companies may have the momentum, power or time to get rid of all obstacles. But the big barriers must be confronted and moved. Action on them is important, both to empower others and to maintain the credibility of the change effort as a whole.

6. Create Short-Term Wins

Since it takes time and much effort to become a learning organization, the change effort risks losing momentum if there are no short-term goals to meet and celebrate. Most people won't stay on the long march unless the journey has some short-term successes.

Creating short-term wins is different from just hoping for them. The learning coalition should actively look for ways to obtain clear performance improvements and to reward the people involved in the efforts with recognition, promotions, and even money.

7. Consolidate Progress Achieved and Push for Continued Movement

After a few months of hard work, the learning organization advocates may be tempted to declare victory when the first signs of transformation occur. While celebrating a win is fine, "declaring the war won can be catastrophic," declares Kotter. "Until changes sink deeply into a company's culture,...new [changes] are fragile and subject to regression (p. 66)."

Instead of declaring victory, leaders of successful learning efforts should use the credibility afforded by short-term gains to tackle even bigger problems. They should go after systems and structures that are not consistent with the new vision and have not been confronted before. They should be paying greater attention to who is promoted, who is hired, and how people are being developed. They understand that becoming a learning organization takes not months, but years; and even then it is never fully finished.

8. Anchor Changes in the Corporation's Culture

In the final analysis, the reality of the learning organization sticks when it becomes institutionalized, when it "seeps into the bloodstream of the corporate body." Until the new behaviors are rooted in social norms and shared values, the subsystems of the learning organization will be subject to retrogression as soon as the pressure for change is removed.

Two factors are particularly important in institutionalizing change in the corporate culture: (1) a conscious attempt to show people how the new approaches, behaviors, and attitudes have helped improve performance, and (2) taking sufficient time to make sure that the next generation of top management does personify the new approach.

Ten Facilitating Factors That Support and Sustain the Learning Organization

Research by the MIT Organizational Learning Center on companies that have successfully built and sustained organizationwide learning reveals that there are ten factors or values that are shared by these organizations.

1. Scanning Imperative

Learning organizations realize that sound learning cannot continue without a solid awareness of the environment in which they are functioning. There must be an interest in external happenings and in the nature of surrounding circumstances. Learning organizations persevere in gathering information about conditions and practices outside their own industry or geographic area. They remain curious about what is out there as opposed to "in here."

2. Performance Gap

Learning organizations see performance shortfalls as opportunities for learning. There are two aspects to this factor:

- As learning organizations look at the differences between targeted outcomes and actual performance and notice a gap, they immediately proceed to experimentation and to the development of new insights and skills. One of the reasons that well-established, long-successful organizations often are not good learning systems is that they experience lengthy periods in which feedback is almost entirely positive. Ironically, this lack of disconfirming evidence is a barrier to learning.

- One or more members of the learning organization visualize something which previously has not been noted. This is important since it often leads to awareness that something needs to be learned or that something believed to be known may not be operable any longer.

3. Concern for Measurement

Learning organizations continue to spend considerable effort in defining and measuring key factors when venturing into new areas. They strive for specific, quantifiable measures. Discourse over metrics is seen as a learning activity and includes such issues as whether the measures are internally or externally focused, the degree of specificity sought, and the use of custom-built or standard measures. The interest in metrics, and the search for the most appropriate ones, is in itself a critical aspect of the learning, almost as much as the learning which accrues from responding to the feedback provided by the metrics.

Whirlpool is an example of a learning organization that carefully measures nonfinancial as well as financial elements. In 1991, CEO David Whitwam announced that the four value-creating objectives of the organization (i.e., cost, quality, productivity, and customer satisfaction) would be publicly announced and measured on an annual basis.

The ongoing measuring of these objectives, Whitwam stated, "would become a powerful tool" in maintaining the learning power in Whirlpool.

4. Experimental Mindset

If learning comes through experience, it follows that the more an organization can plan guided experiences, the more it will learn. Until organizing for production at any stage of the value chain is seen as a learning experiment as well as a production activity, learning will come slowly. Managers in learning companies continue to act like applied research scientists at the same time as they deliver goods and services. Motorola University, for example, has been an experimental venture from its launching and constantly tries out new learning approaches. At Wal-Mart, on any given day, there are about 250 experiments being conducted in their stores in areas such as sales promotion, display, and customer service.

Sustained learning organizations support the practice of trying new things and being curious about how things work. They have the ability to "play" with things and see changes in work processes, policies, and structures as a continuous series of learning opportunities.

5. Climate of Openness

Companies that keep growing as learning organizations realize the importance of the accessibility of information. They keep on expanding open communications within the organization. Problems, errors, and lessons are shared, not hidden. Debate and conflict remain acceptable ways of solving problems. There is a permeability of boundaries around information flow and the degree to which observation opportunity is available to people. Much informal learning that takes place is a part of daily, often unplanned interactions among people. The opportunity to attend meetings with other groups and to see higher levels of management in operation promotes learning. This factor includes the freedom with which people can express their views and the degree of disagreement and debate that is legitimate.

6. Continuous Education

To maintain the high-level power of a learning organization, there must be an ongoing internalization of commitment to lifelong education at all levels of the organization and a clear support for growth and development of all members. This includes not only formal educational programs but also the more pervasive support of any kind of developmental experience for members of the organization.

In addition to training and development activities, there must be a palpable sense that one is never finished learning and practicing. In many ways, this factor is another way of expressing what Peter Senge called "personal mastery."

7. Operational Variety

Learning organizations realize that there are more ways than one to accomplish business objectives and work goals. An organization that supports variation in strategy, policy, process, structure, and personnel will be much more adaptable when unforeseen problems arise. This appreciation of diversity provides more options from which to chose and, perhaps even more importantly, it allows for richer stimulation and interpretation in the consciousness of all organizational members. This variety of methods, procedures, and approaches helps to enhance future learning in a way that a single approach does not make possible.

8. Multiple Advocates or Champions

In successful learning organizations, new ideas and methods can be advanced by employees at all organizational levels. Multiple advocates or champions exist for various learning initiatives. The greater the number of advocates who promote a new idea, the more rapidly and extensively will the learning take place. Moreover, in an effective learning organization, it is possible for any member to be an awareness-enhancing agent or an advocate for new competence development. In this way, both top-down and bottom-up initiatives are made possible.

9. Involved Leadership

Organizational leaders articulate the learning vision and are actively engaged in this actualization. Leaders must remain actively involved in learning programs. The importance of leadership in setting vision that mobilizes enhanced performance is very clear.

Creating vision is not enough. For assimilated, institutionalized organizational learning to occur, leadership at any organizational level must engage in hands-on implementation of the vision. This includes eliminating the layers of management, being visible in the "bowels" of the organization, and being an active early participant in any learning effort. Only through direct involvement that reflects coordination, vision, and integration can leadership obtain important data, a well as provide a powerful role model.

10. Systems Perspective

Maintaining a learning organization requires a systems perspective. Focusing on the interdependence of organizational units and activities is crucial. The organization keeps a broad perspective and thinks in terms of the interdependency of organizational variables. It sees problems and solutions in terms of systemic relationships among processes, and recognizes the connection between unit needs and goals with organizationwide needs and goals.

Caterpillars, Cocoons, and Butterflies—Transitions to a Learning Organization and Global Success

There are several stages and transformations that a company must pass through on its journey to becoming a learning organization. The transformational journey of the caterpillar may serve as an enlightening metaphor.

The caterpillar (i.e., the nonlearning or slow-learning organization) survives and slowly grows to a size and speed appropriate for caterpillars. It is limited in movement and can crawl in only one direction, usually crunching back slightly in order to gradually proceed forward. It is subject to being devoured by predators (other organizations) who are more agile and powerful. Moving a little faster or changing colors (even giving the caterpillar tiny legs or little wings (reengineering, TQM) would not enable the caterpillar it to reach its full potential; it is still earthbound.

At some point, therefore, the caterpillar enters into a cocoon (chrysalis) where an incredible process takes place. The caterpillar quite literally dissolves into a messy ooze, and then the raw protoplasm reaggregates (reforming, reengineering, restructuring, refocusing) as a butterfly.

Having gone through this messy, challenging process, the caterpillar emerges with the beauty and power of the butterfly, which can fly in all directions—up and down, sideways and forward and backward, loop-to-loop. The butterfly is able to flow with the wind or find safety from it.

So too the transition from a weak nonlearning company to the powerful learning organization that has an enhanced organizational capacity to change and transform itself. The learning organization empowers its people, integrates quality initiatives with quality of work life, creates free space for learning, encourages collaboration and sharing the gains, promotes inquiry, and creates continuous learning opportunities. Learning in learning organizations changes perceptions, behaviors, beliefs, mental models, strategies, policies, and procedures in people and organizations. All five subsystems serve as the wings to carry the organization skyward!

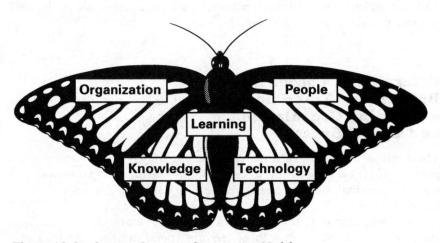

Figure 10-1. Systems Learning Organization Model.

The six superstars of organizational learning explored in this book are companies who have gone from being reasonably competent caterpillars to being beautiful, graceful powerful butterflies. They have metamorphosed and adapted themselves to the changing environment and workplace, to changing workers and customers, and have now become leaders in their respective industries as well as global success stories.

Learning organizations are where global success is more possible, where quality is more assured, and where energetic and talented people want to be. Best of success in building your learning organization!

Appendix

Learning Organization Profile*

*Copyright Global Learning Associates and Dr. Michael J. Marquardt.

LEARNING ORGANIZATION PROFILE

Below is a list of various statements about your organization. Read each statement carefully and decide the *extent* to which it actually applies to your organization. Use the following scale:

4 = applies totally
3 = applies to a great extent
2 = applies to a moderate extent
1 = applies to little or no extent

I. Learning Dynamics: Individual, Group/Team, and Organizational

In this organization…

_____ 1. We see continuous learning by all employees as a high business priority.

_____ 2. We are encouraged and expected to manage our own learning and development.

_____ 3. People avoid distortion of information and blocking of communication channels through skills such as active listening and effective feedback.

_____ 4. Individuals are trained and coached in learning how to learn.

_____ 5. We use various accelerated learning methodologies (e.g., mindmapping, mnemonics, peripherals, imagery, music, etc.).

_____ 6. People expand knowledge through adaptive, anticipatory, and creative learning approaches.

_____ 7. Teams and individuals use the action-learning process (that is, learning from careful reflection on the problem or situation, and applying it to future actions).

_____ 8. Teams are encouraged to learn from one another and to share learnings in a variety of ways (e.g., via electronic bulletin boards, printed newsletters, intergroup meetings, etc.).

_____ 9. People are able to think and act with a comprehensive, systems approach.

_____ 10. Teams receive training in how to work and learn in groups.

_____ Total Score: Learning Dynamics (maximum score: 40)

II. Organization Transformation: Vision, Culture, Strategy, and Structure

In this organization...

_____ 1. The importance of being a learning organization is understood throughout the organization.

_____ 2. Top-level management supports the vision of a learning organization.

_____ 3. There is a climate that supports and recognizes the importance of learning.

_____ 4. We are committed to continuous learning for improvement.

_____ 5. We learn from failures as well as successes.

_____ 6. We reward people and teams for learning and helping others learn.

_____ 7. Learning opportunities are incorporated into operations and programs.

_____ 8. We design ways to share knowledge and enhance learning throughout the organization (e.g., systematic job rotation across divisions, structured on-the-job learning systems).

_____ 9. The organization is streamlined, with few levels of management, to maximize communication and learning across levels.

_____ 10. We coordinate on the basis of goals and learning rather than maintaining separation in terms of fixed departmental boundaries.

_____ Total Score: Organization Transformation (maximum score: 40)

III. People Empowerment: Employee, Manager, Customer, Alliances, Partners, and Community

In this organization...

_____ 1. We strive to develop an empowered work force that is able and committed to qualitative learning and performance.

_____ 2. Authority is decentralized and delegated so as to equal one's responsibility and learning capability.

_____ 3. Managers and nonmanagers work together in partnership, to learn and solve problems together.

_____ 4. Managers take on the roles of coaching, mentoring, and facilitating learning.

_____ 5. Managers generate and enhance learning opportunities as well as encourage experimentation and reflection on what was learned so that new knowledge can be used.

_____ 6. We actively share information with our customers, to obtain their ideas and inputs in order to learn and improve services/products.

_____ 7. We give customers and suppliers opportunities to participate in learning and training activities.

_____ 8. Learning from partners (subcontractors, teammates, and suppliers) is maximized through up-front planning of resources and strategies devoted to knowledge and skill acquisition.

_____ 9. We participate in joint learning events with suppliers, community groups, professional associations, and academic institutions.

_____ 10. We actively seek learning partners among customers, vendors, and suppliers.

_____ Total Score: People Empowerment (maximum score: 40)

IV. Knowledge Management: Acquisition, Creation, Storage/Retrieval, and Transfer/Utilization

In this organization...

_____ 1. People actively seek information that improves the work of the organization.

_____ 2. We have accessible systems for collecting internal and external information.

_____ 3. People monitor trends outside our organization by looking at what others do (e.g., benchmarking best practices, attending conferences, and examining published research).

_____ 4. People are trained in the skills of creative thinking and experimentation.

_____ 5. We often create demonstration projects where new ways of developing a product and/or delivering a service are tested.

_____ 6. Systems and structures exist to ensure that important knowledge is coded, stored, and made available to those who need and can use it.

_____ 7. People are aware of the need to retain important organizational learnings and share such knowledge with others.

_____ 8. Cross-functional teams are used to transfer important learning across groups, departments, and divisions.

_____ 9. We continue to develop new strategies and mechanisms for sharing learning throughout the organization.

_____ 10. We support specific areas, units, and projects that generate knowledge by providing people with learning opportunities.

_____ Total Score: Knowledge Management (maximum score: 40)

V. Technology Application: Information Systems, Technology-Based Learning, and Electronic Performance Support Systems

In this organization...

_____ 1. Learning is facilitated by effective and efficient computer-based information systems.

_____ 2. People have ready access to the information highway (local area networks, internet, on-line, etc.).

_____ 3. Learning facilities (e.g., training and conference rooms) incorporate electronic multimedia support and a learning environment based on the powerful integration of art, color, music, and visuals.

_____ 4. People have available to them computer-assisted learning programs and electronic job aids (e.g., just-in-time and flowcharting software).

_____ 5. We use groupware technology to manage group processes (e.g., project management, team process, meeting management).

_____ 6. We support just-in-time learning, a system that integrates high-technology learning systems, coaching, and actual work on the job into a single, seamless process.

_____ 7. Our electronic support performance systems enable us to learn and to do our work better.

_____ 8. We design and tailor our electronic performance support systems to meet our learning needs.

_____ 9. People have full access to the data they need to do their jobs effectively.

_____ 10. We can adapt software systems to collect, code, store, create, and transfer information in ways best suited to meet our needs.

_____ Total Score: Technology Application (maximum score: 40)

Grand Total for Five Subsystems:————(maximum score: 200)

Glossary

Many special terms are used in defining and describing learning organizations. In addition, there are some terms which assume a different connotation in reference to organizational learning.

Accelerated Learning: A system of learning designed to improve rate of learning and overall retention by incorporating creative, sensory-rich learning techniques.

Action Learning: Deliberate, conscious effort to review and reflect on action of the individual or the organization. Developed by Reginald Revans, it is the combination of P (programmed or already-existing information) plus Q (questioning of existing information to learn from and apply it).

Action-Reflection Learning: A form of action learning that involves a systematic reflection or review of a person's or team's action to determine what can be learned from it (a form of action learning).

Adaptive Learning: An individual's or organization's learning from experience and reflection.

Anergy: The whole is less than the sum of its parts. For example, $2 + 2 = 3$. Anergy is the opposite of synergy.

Anticipatory Learning: An individual's or organization's learning in order to meet needs that are projected for the future. The anticipatory learning sequence is vision-reflection-action.

Competency: An area of capability that enables a person or organization to perform.

Competitiveness Skills: Skills that provide for future needs; includes systems thinking, team learning, visioning, mental models.

Computer-Based Learning: Umbrella term that includes all forms of use of computers in support of learning (*see also* Technology-Based Learning).

Continuous Learning Culture: The milieu or environment in which people are encouraged and enabled to learn in an ongoing, continuous basis.

Core Competencies: Companies structured according to competencies (what they do best) instead of according to product or market.

Dialogue: Denotes the high level of listening and communication between people. It requires the free and creative exploration of subtle issues, a deep listening to one another and suspending of one's own views. The discipline of dialogue involves learning how to recognize the patterns of interaction in teams that promote or undermine learning. For example, the patterns of defensiveness are often deeply ingrained in how a group of people or an organization operates. If unrecognized or avoided, they undermine learning. If recognized and surfaced creatively, they can actually accelerate learning. Dialogue is the critical medium for connecting, inventing, and coordinating learning and action in the workplace.

Double-Loop Learning: In-depth organizational learning that looks at organizational norms and structures that cause the organization to function in the way it does. Double-loop learning, developed by Chris Argyris, questions the system itself and why errors or successes occurred in the first place.

Duetero Learning: An organization's or individual's learning from critical reflection on taken-for-granted assumptions; an examination of how the learning is or is not occurring.

Electronic Performance Support Systems (EPSS): Systems that use databases (text, visual, or audio) and knowledge bases to capture, store, and distribute information throughout the organization so as to help workers reach the highest level of performance in the fastest possible time, with the least personnel support. The systems consists of several components including, but not limited to, interactive training, productivity and application software, and expert and feedback systems.

Explicit Knowledge: Formal, systematic, and easily shared knowledge (in contrast to tacit knowlege).

Generative Organizational Learning: The learning that an organization generates or creates itself from its own reflection, analysis, or creativity.

Group/Team Learning: Alludes to the increase in knowledge, skills, and competencies which are accomplished by and within groups.

Individual Learning: Refers to the change of skills, insights, knowledge, attitudes, and values acquired by a person through self-study, technology-based instruction, and observation.

Informate: The use of computer-generated data collected during implementation for planing and decision making. For example, the supermarket checkout data scan provides information (what foods were bought, who buys what, when they were bought, etc.) that enables the store to plan advertising, hiring, purchasing, and inventory control.

Know-How: Value-added information.

Know-How Company: An organization that produces and sells information, ideas, and complex problem solving to others. Key features include nonstandardization, creativity, and high dependence on knowledge of individuals.

Know-How Workers (also called gold-collar employees): Skilled and creative employees primarily involved in problem solving, problem identifying, and strategic brokering activities for outside customers. Know-how workers may includes programmers, consultants, physicians, accountants, engineers, and others.

Knowledge Architecture: The repository for shared knowledge and collective intelligence that is organized for easy access by any staff member, any time, and from anywhere. For example, a database that collects key learning of individuals or an on-line newsletter that systematically gathers, organizes, and disseminates the collective knowledge of the organization members.

Knowledge Acquisition: The process by which existing knowledge is collected or obtained. Knowledge can be purchased, borrowed, or stolen.

Knowledge Creation: The development of new knowledge through innovation, problem solving, insights, or adaptation.

Knowledge Retrieval: The acquisition of knowledge that is already in the organization and stored in various systems, such as human, computer, and written documentation.

Knowledge Storage: The coding and preserving of the organization's valued knowledge for easy access by any organizational member, at any time, and from any place.

Knowledge Transfer: Process by which information is moved and shared throughout the organization through individuals and groups across various functions. This can be done through personal, mechanical, and electronic means.

Learning Organization: A company that learns powerfully and collectively and is continually transforming itself to better manage and use knowledge for corporate success; it empowers people within and outside the organization to learn as they work, and it utilizes technology to maximize learning and production.

Mental Model: One's image of reality; in organizational learning, refers to a person's values and beliefs regarding learning.

Mentofacturing: The production of products and services through the efforts of the mind, Latin *mento*. Mentofacturing stands in contrast to manufacturing, which is derived from the Latin *manus* meaning hand.

Metalogue: A high level of dialogue in which a group thinks and creates together.

Mission Statement: The operational, ethical, and financial guiding direction of a company; it articulate the goals, dreams, behavior, culture, and strategies of companies

Open-Space Technology: An innovative approach, developed by Harrison Owen, to enhance individual and group performance in which up to 400 people self-organize and self manage multiday meetings and conferences around complex issues.

Organizational Architecture: Structural form of organizations that evolves around autonomous work teams and strategic alliances.

Organizational Learning: Refers to "how" learning occurs on an organizationwide basis (as opposed to *learning organization* which describes the "what"). Refers to the systems, principles, and characteristics of organizations that learn as a collective entity.

Organization-Level Learning: The third level of learning in a learning organization (*see also* individual learning and group/team learning). Represents the enhanced intellectual and productive capability gained through corporatewide commitment and opportunity to continuous improvement. It differs from individual and group/team learning in two basic respects. First, organizational learning occurs through the shared insights, knowledge, and mental models of members of the organization. Second, organizational learning builds on past knowledge and experience—that is, on organizational memory, which depends on institutional mechanisms (e.g., policies, strategies, and explicit models) used to retain knowledge.

Organization Memory: System established by the organization to store knowledge for future use. Memory is retrievable and can be in individuals or in technology.

Organization Transformation: Large-scale change in the organization that includes mission, values, structure, and systems.

Patterns of Organizational Learning: Learning patterns that are based on tacit and explicit knowledge and their interaction. Ikujiro Nonaka identifies four patterns: tacit to tacit, explicit to explicit, tacit to explicit, and explicit to tacit.

Personal Mastery: High level of proficiency in a subject or skill area.

Quantum Improvement: Doing entirely different things better (versus gradual improvement, which is greater improvement along a continuum).

Reengineering: Restructuring of organizations around outcomes, and not tasks or functions. It involves a fundamental rethinking and remaking of business systems that urges an overhaul of job designs, organization structures, and management systems. Work should be organized around outcomes, not tasks or functions (e.g., streamlining structures to decrease levels that filter knowledge transfer).

Single-Loop Learning: Gaining information to stabilize and maintain the existing operational systems.

Social Architecture: The cultural, symbolic relationship orientation of the organization that enhances learning by encouraging teams, self-management, empowerment, and sharing. Social architecture is the opposite of a closed, rigid, bureaucratic architecture.

Societal Learning: The fourth level of learning (individual, group, and organization being the first three) in which the community is learning as an entity.

Synergy: Where the sum is greater than the parts; for example, $2 + 2 = 5$.

Systems Learning: Learning which sees interrelationships and the whole as more than the sum of the parts.

Systems Thinking: A conceptual framework with a body of knowledge and tools that makes complex patterns clearer and shows how to change them effectively.

Tacit Knowledge: Knowledge that is held inside and is difficult to express (in contrast to explicit knowledge).

Team Learning: Learning in which the group or team is learning as an single entity.

Technological Architecture: The supporting, integrated set of technical processes, systems, and structure for collaboration, coaching, coordination, and other knowledge skills. Technological architecture may include such electronic tools and advanced methods for learning as computer conferencing, simulation software, and computer supported collaboration, all of which work to create knowledge freeways.

Technology-Based Learning: Video, audio, and computer-based multimedia training for the delivery and sharing of knowledge and skills away from the job site.

Training: Instructional experiences for learners planned and delivered by trainers, generally in a formal setting (as distinguished from "learning," where change is the responsibility of the learner).

Vision Statement: The intended hope and long-term goal for an organization; for learning organizations, a picture of what the organization wishes to look like relative to learning.

Bibliography

Argyris, Chris: "Double Loop Learning in Organizations." *Harvard Business Review*, September–October 1987, pp. 11–25.

———: "Teaching Smart People How to Learn." *Harvard Business Review*, May–June 1991, pp. 99–109.

———: *Knowledge for Action.* San Francisco: Jossey-Bass, 1993.

———, and D. A. Schon: *Organizational Learning: A Theory of Action Perspective.* Reading, Mass.: Addison-Wesley, 1978.

Bateson, Gregory: *Steps to an Ecology of Mind.* New York: Ballantine Books, 1971.

Beck, Michael: "Learning Organizations—How to Create Them." *Industrial & Commercial Training*, 21(3), pp. 21–28.

Bennett, K. J., and Michael O'Brien: "The Building Blocks of the Learning Organization." *Training*, June 1994, pp. 41–49.

Birchard, Bill: "The Call for Full Disclosure." *CFO*, December 1994, pp. 31–42.

Bogan, Christopher E., and Michael J. English: "Benchmarking of Best Practices." *Quality Digest*, August 1994, pp. 52–62.

Bower, David: "The Learning Organization: A Rover Perspective." *Executive Development*, 6(2), pp. 3–6.

Brinkerhoff, Robert, and Stephen Gill: *The Learning Alliance: Systems Thinking in Human Resource Development.* San Francisco: Jossey-Bass, 1994.

Broad, Mary, and John Newstrom: *Transfer of Training.* Reading, Mass.: Addison-Wesley, 1992.

Brookfield, Stephen D.: *Understanding and Facilitating Adult Learning.* San Francisco: Jossey-Bass, 1986.

Brown, J. S., and P. Duguid: "Organization Learning and Communities-in-Practice." *Organization Science*, 2(1), pp. 40–57.

Byrd, Mary: "Learning Organizations—A Model for the Future." Unpublished, 1992.

Byrne, John: "Management's New Gurus." *Business Week*, August 31, 1992, pp. 44–52.

Calvert, Gene, S. Mobley, and Lisa Marshall: "Grasping the Learning Organization." *Training and Development*, June 1994, pp. 39–43.

Campbell, Robert, and David Monson: "Building a Goal-Based Scenario Learning Environment." *Educational Technology*, November–December 1994, pp. 9–14.

Chawla, Sarita, and John Renesch (eds.): *Learning Organizations: Developing Cultures for Tomorrow's Workplace.* Portland, Oreg.: Productivity Press, 1995.

Daft, R. L., and G. Huber: "How Organizations Learn: A Communications Framework." *Research in the Sociology of Organizations,* V. 5, 1987, pp. 1–36.

Davidow, William H., and Michael Malone: *The Virtual Corporation.* New York: HarperCollins Publishers, 1992.

DeGeus, A. P.: "Planning as Learning." *Harvard Business Review,* March–April 1988, pp. 70–74.

Dixon, Nancy: "Organizational Learning: A Review of the Literature with Implications for HRD Professionals." *Human Resource Development Quarterly,* 3(1), pp. 29–49.

Dixon, Nancy: *The Organizational Learning Cycle.* New York: McGraw-Hill, 1994.

Drucker, Peter: "The New Society of Organizations." *Harvard Business Review,* September–October 1992, pp. 95–104.

Dumanaine, Brian: "Mr. Learning Organization." *Fortune,* October 17, 1994, pp. 146–157.

Easterby-Smith, M.: "Creating a Learning Organization." *Personnel Review,* May 1990, pp. 24–28.

Fiol, C. M., and M. A. Lyles: "Organizational Learning," *Academy of Management Review,* 10(4), pp. 803–813.

Froiland, Paul: "Action Learning: Taming Real Problems in Real Time." *Training,* January 1994, pp. 27–33.

Galagan, Patricia: "The Learning Organization Made Plain." *Training and Development Journal,* 45(10), pp. 37–44.

Garvin, David: "Building a Learning Organization." *Harvard Business Review,* July–August, 1993, pp. 78–79.

Gery, Gloria: *Electronic Performance Support Systems.* Cambridge, Mass.: Ziff Institute, 1991.

Gill, Mary Jane, and David Meier: "Accelerated Learning Takes Off." *Training and Development,* January 1989, pp. 28–32.

Gill, Stephen: "Shifting Gears for High Performance." *Training and Development,* May 1995, pp. 25–31.

Hammer, Michael, and James Champy: *Reengineering the Corporation.* New York: HarperCollins Publishers, 1993.

Handy, Charles: *The Age of Unreason.* London: Basic, 1989.

Harman, Willis, and John Hormann: *Creative Work: The Constructive Role of Business in a Transforming Society.* An Institute of Noetic Science Publication, Knowledge Systems, Inc., 1990.

Honold, L.: "The Power of Learning at Johnsonville Foods." *Training,* April 1991, pp. 55–58.

Isaacs, William: "Taking Flight: Dialogue, Collective Thinking, and Organizational Learning." *Organizational Dynamics,* Autumn 1993, pp. 24–39.

Jaccaci, August: "The Social Architecture of A Learning Organization." *Training and Development Journal,* 43(11), pp. 49–51.

Johnston, William: "Global Workforce 2000: The New World Labor Market." *Harvard Business Review,* March–April 1991, pp. 115–127.

Jones, Alan, and Chris Hendry: *The Learning Organization*. Coventry, U.K., HRD Partnership, 1992.

Kearns, David, and David Nadler: *Prophets in the Dark: How Xerox Reinvented Itself and Beat Back the Japanese*. New York: Harper Business, 1992.

Kiechel, Walter: "The Organization that Learns." *Fortune*, March 12, 1990, pp. 133–136.

Kim, Daniel: "The Link Between Individual and Organizational Learning." *Sloan Management Review*, Fall 1993, pp. 37–50.

Kline, Peter, and Bernard Saunder: *Ten Steps to a Learning Organization*. Arlington, Va.: Great Ocean Publishers, 1993.

Kofman, F., and Peter Senge: "Communities of Commitment: The Heart of Learning Organizations." *Organizational Dynamics*, Autumn 1993, pp. 5–23.

Kotter, John P.: "Leading Change: Why Transformation Efforts Fail." *Harvard Business Review*, March–April 1995, pp. 59–67.

Leonard-Barton, D.: "The Factory as a Learning Laboratory." *Sloan Management Review*, Fall 1992, pp. 23–38.

Lessem, Ronnie: *Business as a Learning Community*. New York: McGraw-Hill, 1993.

Levin, Scott A.: *Basics of Electronic Performance Support Systems*. Alexandria, Va.: ASTD Press, 1995.

Marquardt, Michael J.: "Building a Global Learning Organization." *Industry and Higher Education*, August 1995, pp. 217–226.

———, and Skipton Leonard: "Building a Learning Organization: An Essential Key to Gaining Competitive Advantage in the Global 90's." *Corporate Psychology*, April 1994, pp. 1–2.

———, and Angus Reynolds: *The Global Learning Organization*. Burr Ridge, Ill.: Irwin Professional Publishing, 1994.

Marsick, Victoria (ed.): *Learning in the Workplace*. New York: Croom Helm, 1987.

———, Lars Cederholm, Ernie Turner, and Ton Pearson. "Action-Reflection Learning." *Training and Development*, August 1992, pp. 63–66.

Maruca, Regina Faxio: "The Right Way to Go Global: An Interview with Whirlpool CEO David Whitwam." *Harvard Business Review*, March–April 1994, pp. 134–145.

Mayo, Andrew, and Elizabeth Lank: *The Power of Learning*. Plymouth, England: IPD Publishing, 1995.

Meister, Jeanne: *Corporate Quality Universities: Lessons for Building a World-Class Workforce*. Burr Ridge, Ill.: Irwin Professional Publishing, 1993.

Mellander, Klass: *Lifelong Learning*. Homewood, Ill.: Business One Irwin, 1993.

Michael, Donald: *On Learning to Plan—and Planning to Learn*. San Francisco: Jossey–Bass, 1989.

Mills, Daniel, and Bruce Friesen: "The Learning Organization." *European Management Journal*, 10(2), pp. 146–156.

Morris, Linda: "Learning Organizations: Settings for Developing Adults." (In Demick, Jack, and Patrice Miller (eds.), *Development in the Workplace*. Hillsdale, N.J.: Lawrence Earlbaum Associates. Inc., 1993.

Morton, Michael (ed.): *The Corporation of the 1990's*. New York: Oxford University Press, 1991.

Nevis, Edwin C., Anthony J. DiBella, and Janet Gould: "Organizations as Learning Systems." The Learning Company Conference, Andover, Mass., November 6–9, 1994.

Nonaka, Ikujiro: "The Knowledge-Creating Company," *Harvard Business Review*, 69(6), pp. 96–104.

———, and Hirotaka Takeuchi: *The Knowledge-Creating Company*. New York: Oxford University Press, 1995.

Nowakowski, Alan: "Reengineering Education at Andersen Consulting." *Educational Technology*, November–December 1994, pp. 3–8.

O'Brien, Michael J., and J. Kremer-Bennett: "The 12 Building Blocks of the Learning Organization." *Training*, June 1994, pp. 41–49.

Oster, Patrick, and John Rossant: "Call It Worldpool." *Business Week*, November 28, 1994, pp. 70–71.

Owen, Harrison: *Riding the Tiger: Doing Business in a Transforming World*. Potomac, Md.: Abbott Publishing, 1991.

———: *The Business of Learning*. (A newsletter sent by Owen to colleagues).

Pascale, Richard: *Managing on the Edge*. New York: Simon and Schuster, 1990.

Pedler, Mike (ed.): *Action Learning in Practice*. Hants, England: Gower, 1991.

———, John Burgoyne, and Tom Boydell: *The Learning Company: A Strategy for Sustainable Development*. London: McGraw-Hill, 1991.

Peters, Tom: *Liberation Management*. New York: Alfred Knopf, 1992.

Peters, Tom, and Robert Waterman: *In Search of Excellence*. New York: Harper and Row, 1982.

Por, George: "What is a Corporate Learning Expedition?" Paper presented at Collaboration in Social Architecture, June 20–21, Cambridge, Mass., 1991.

Port, Otis: "Learning from the Competition—How Companies Use Benchmarking," *Business Week*, November 30, 1992, pp. 74–75.

Pucik, V.: "Strategic Alliances, Organizational Learning, and Competitive Advantage: The HRD Agenda." *Human Resource Management*, 27(1), pp. 77–93.

Quinn, Brian: *The Intelligent Organization*. New York: Free Press, 1992.

Ray, Michael: "The Emerging New Paradigm in Business." In John Renesch (ed.), *New Traditions in Business Spirit & Leadership in the 21st Century*. San Francisco: New Leaders Publications, 1991.

Raybould, Barry: *Making EPSS Work for Your Organization*. Alexandria, Va.: ASTD Press, 1995.

Redding, John: *Strategic Readiness: The Making of the Learning Organization*. San Francisco: Jossey-Bass, 1994.

Reich, Robert: *The Work of Nations*. New York: Random House, 1991.

Revans, Reginald: *Action Learning: New Techniques for Management*. London: Blond & Briggs, 1980.

Savage, Charles: *Fifth Generation Management*. Burlington, Mass.: Digital Press, 1990.

Schein, Edgar: "On Dialogue, Culture, and Organizational Learning." *Organizational Dynamics*, Autumn 1993, pp. 40–51.

———: "How Can Organizations Learn Faster?" Address to World Economics Forum, 1992.

Schwandt, David: "Thoughts on Organization Learning Theory," Unpublished, 1994.

Senge, Peter: *The Fifth Discipline*, New York: Doubleday, 1990.

———: "The Leader's New Work: Building Learning Organizations." *Sloan Management Review*, 32(1), pp. 7–23.

——— et al.: *The Fifth Discipline Fieldbook: Strategies and Tools for Building a Learning Organization*. New York: Doubleday, 1994.

Shrivastava, Paul: "Learning Structures for Top Management." *Human Systems Management*, 6(1), pp. 35–44.

Stata, Ray: "Organizational Learning—The Key to Management Innovation." *Sloan Management Review*, 30(3), pp. 63–74.

Stewart, Thomas: "Brainpower," *Fortune*, June 3, 1991, pp. 44–60).

Sveiby, Karl, and Tom Lloyd: *Managing Knowhow*. London: Bloombury, 1987.

Taylor, Sally: "Managing a Learning Environment." *Personnel Management*, October 1992, pp. 54–57.

The Virtual Organization: *Business Week*, February 8, 1993, p. 100.

Tobin, Daniel R.: *Re-Educating the Corporation: Foundations for the Learning Organization*. Essex Junction, Colo.: Oliver Wright Publications, 1993.

Toffler, Alvin: *Powershift*. New York: Bantam, 1990.

Veilleux, Rene: "A Nationwide Descriptive Study About Learning in US Businesses as Perceived by Human Resource Development Practitioners." Unpublished doctoral dissertation, George Washington University, 1995.

Verity, John, and Robert Hof: "Planet Internet." *Business Week*, April 3, 1995, pp. 118–124.

Verlander, E. G.: "Executive Education for Managing Complex Organizational Learning." *Human Resource Planning*, 15(2), pp. 1–16.

Vogt, Judith, and Kenneth Murrell: *Empowerment in Organizations*. San Diego: Pfeiffer & Company, 1993.

Watkins, Karen, and Victoria Marsick: *Sculpting the Learning Organization*. San Francisco: Jossey-Bass, 1993.

Waterman, Robert: *The Renewal Factor: How the Best Get and Keep the Competitive Edge*. New York: Bantam Books, 1987.

Webber, Alan. "What's So New About the New Economy," *Harvard Business Review*, January–February 1993, pp. 24–42.

Weik, Karl E.: "The Nontraditional Quality of Organizational Learning." *Organization Science*, 2(1), pp. 116–124.

Wheatley, Margaret: *Leadership and the New Science*. San Francisco: Berrett-Koehler Publishers, 1992.

Wick, Calhoun, and Lu Stanton Leon: *The Learning Edge*. New York: McGraw-Hill, 1993.

Willis, V. J.: "The New Learning Organization: Should There Be a Chief Learning Officer in the House?" *Human Resource Development Quarterly*, 2(2), 181–187.

Wilson, William: "Video Training and Testing Supports Customer Service Goals." *Personnel Journal*, June 1994, pp. 46–51.

Wriston, Walter: *The Twilight of Sovereignty: How the Information Revolutions is Transforming the World*. New York: Charles Scribner & Sons, 1992.

Zinno, Vincent: "The Message of Multimedia." *Human Resource Executive,* February 1995, pp. 31–34.

Zuboff, Shoshana: *In the Age of the Smart Machine: The Future of Work and Power.* New York: Basic Books, 1988.

Index

About the Author

Michael J. Marquardt is a professor at George Washington University, home of the Academy for Applied Research in Organizational Learning. He is also President of Global Learning Associates which assists companies throughout the world on their journey toward becoming learning organizations. Dr. Marquardt has been a keynote speaker at several international conferences on the topic of the learning organization and is the author of over 30 books and professional articles in the field of organizational development and learning.